The Observer's Pocket Series

COMMERCIAL VEHICLES

About the book

Following four successful editions of the *Observer's Book of Commercial Vehicles* this is the first to specialize solely in trucks. It contains examples of fire appliances, dumptrucks, heavy-haulage tractors, special-purpose chassis and general goods vehicles of all sorts from the majority of the world's manufacturers. The background history of each firm is briefly described along with details of its current products. The book contains some 239 photographs and will be of considerable interest to truck and component manufacturers as well as operators, drivers and enthusiasts.

About the author

Nick Baldwin has been closely involved with trucks for over twenty years. He was apprenticed with the Rover Co Ltd and afterwards studied continental truck operation in Switzerland. He has worked for various transport magazines including *Autocar, Commercial Vehicles, Motor Transport* and *Old Motor* and is a regular contributor to *Truck*. He has compiled *Farm Tractors* and *Trucks of the Sixties and Seventies* in Warne's Transport Library series and is a partner in the transport book publishing firm of Marshall, Harris and Baldwin Ltd, London. In his few spare moments he collects and restores old trucks.

The Observer's Book of

COMMERCIAL VEHICLES

COMPILED BY
NICK BALDWIN

DESCRIBING MODELS FROM
135 COMPANIES
WITH 239 ILLUSTRATIONS

FREDERICK WARNE
LONDON

Published by Frederick Warne (Publishers) Ltd, London
First published 1967
New editions 1971, 1974, 1978, 1981

Abbreviations and Glossary

Engines: All are in-line engines unless stated (eg V-6 is two banks of three cylinders). All are four-stroke and water-cooled unless specifically mentioned. Wherever possible power output is quoted net installed in both brake horse power (bhp) and kilowatts (0.746 kW equals 1 bhp). Swept engine volume is recorded in cubic centimetres and inches (cc and cu ins). Fuels are petrol (US: gasoline), derv/diesel and liquefied petroleum gas (LPG).

Cab: Forward and normal control (US: cabover and conventional). BBC indicates measurement from bumper to back of cab. Tilt cab means that it hinges forward to give mechanical access and grp stands for glass-reinforced plastic.

Chassis and transmission: Number of transmission speeds quoted refers to forward gears unless stated otherwise. IFS/IRS (independent front/rear suspension on light vehicles) 4×4, 6×2 etc indicates number of wheels (double tyres count as one wheel) first, followed by number driven. Weights quoted are gross train weight (GTW)—the maximum all-up weight that can be towed and carried; gross combined weight (GCW)—truck with semi-trailer; and gross vehicle weight (GVW\—total weight of rigid vehicle with load. Sometimes the weights quoted are the legal maximum in the country of origin (the plated weight in Britain) and sometimes the designed maximum.

ISBN 0 7232 1619 3

Printed in Great Britain by
Butler & Tanner Ltd, Frome and London

1474·980

INTRODUCTION

We have had an overwhelming response from manufacturers wishing to be included in this new edition and to fit them all in we have had to exclude the engine section which previously appeared. The result of these changes is a massive increase in the number of truck makes from all over the world which can be given coverage.

Every firm that supplied photographs and particulars of internal combustion engined trucks over one ton capacity, by April 1980, appears in the following pages plus a few whose model ranges have not changed appreciably since the 1978 edition. All the world's major manufacturers are listed plus the great majority of smaller specialized builders, whose ranks have grown considerably in recent years, especially in developing countries. A list of all the companies and individuals who have helped with this edition would be almost as long as the book itself, but our thanks to everyone, and particularly everyone at transport book publishers Marshall, Harris and Baldwin Ltd in London, to Frank Whalley at Seddon-Atkinson, Trevor Longcroft at Leyland, Neville O'Keefe at Motor Panels the Coventry cab makers, Phil Reed at the British end of Cummins Engines, to American expert Elliot Kahn and to Nick Georgano, whose *Complete Encyclopaedia of Commercial Vehicles* had been invaluable for checking historical facts.

AB

Autocamioane Brasov
Str. Poienelor nr. 5
Cod 2200 Brasov
Romania

The AB state-owned truck factory at Brasov produced 34,000 vehicles in 1978 and these were sold under the name ROMAN (built under licence from MAN), DAC and Bucegi. These covered the payload range of 2.5 to 25 tonnes and above 5 tonnes all were diesel powered. The Romanian industry also produces lighter vans, trucks and utility vehicles with two- and four-wheel drive under the names ARO and TV, the latter being sold in Britain as Tudor.

TV 12F or Tudor Panel Van has Peugeot 70 bhp, 2.1-litre diesel or ARO 80 bhp, 2.5-litre petrol engines and is for 1390 kg loads. It has a four-speed, synchromesh gearbox and a 4×4 version is available.

ROMAN 19.215 DFS built under MAN licence for operation at 38,000 kg GTW. It has a 10,344 cc, six-cylinder, 158 kW (215 bhp) diesel and six-speed, constant-mesh gearbox. A tilt cab is fitted. Other ROMAN models are available for payloads of 7850 kg to 25 tonnes.

DAC 665 T has 6×6 and 5-tonne capacity. It uses the same engine and gearbox as the ROMAN 19.215 but with the addition of a two-speed transfer box. As a military truck it can climb 60% gradients and can be fitted with a winch and on-the-move tyre pressure adjuster. DAC also makes normal-control 4×2 and 4×4 trucks with Perkins engines.

ALFA-ROMEO

Alfa-Romeo SpA
Via Gattamelata 45
Milan 20149
Italy

Alfa-Romeo have produced trucks since 1930 but have dropped out of all but the lighter weight ranges since the sixties. Since 1967 their van and truck designs have tended to stem from Saviem/Renault whilst in 1974 Alfa-Romeo, Saviem and Fiat jointly formed Sofim to produce a common range of diesel engines in Italy which are used in the AR8 range. The lighter F12/A12 models use Perkins 4.108 diesels. The company has been state controlled for many years.

AR8 models range in payload capacity from 1370 to 2080 kgs (with basic sided truck body). This is the **35 AR8 Furgone** with 11.5 cu m body. It has a 2445 cc, four-cylinder Sofim diesel developing 53 kW (72 bhp) or a 1290 cc, 52.5 bhp, Alfa petrol engine. It has independent suspension on all wheels and front disc brakes.

ALM

Les Ateliers de Construction Mécanique
  de l'Atlantique (ACMAT)
Saint-Nazaire
Brittany
France

ALM all-wheel drive vehicles have been made since 1958, mostly for military purposes. A similar fibreglass front to the one shown has been used from the outset. All have Ford petrol or Perkins diesel engines and 4×4 and 6×6 models are currently produced with payloads of 2.5 tonnes and upwards.

640 SM2 has 180 bhp, Perkins V-8 diesel engine. Its axles, transfer box and synchromesh gearbox are by ACMAT. A military 6×6 is shown carrying a refrigerated container.

AMERICAN-COLEMAN

The American-Coleman Company
PO Box 72
Littleton
Colorado 80160
USA

Founded in 1922, to make driven front axles to convert
4×2 trucks to 4×4, Coleman soon began to assemble
complete vehicles for military and highway maintenance
purposes. Since World War II it has made a large number
of aircraft tugs and in 1948 changed its name to American-
Coleman. To its range of special-purpose vehicles and
tugs in 1977 it added the Champion range of dock spotters
(ro-ro tractors) and also makes 4×4 and four-wheel steer
tractors for a number of on- and off-road haulage purposes.

G-40 Towing Tractor is available with various engine
and transmission options and can steer on front, back
or both axles simultaneously. In the latter case it can
turn in under 30 ft or crab steer. With 4×4 it is used
for snow ploughing and heavy haulage.

AMERICAN LAFRANCE

American LaFrance
Division of ATO
100 East LaFrance Street
Elmira
New York 14902
USA

The origins of American LaFrance go back to 1832. The company has made self-propelled motor fire engines since 1910 and its first forward-control (cab in front of engine) model in 1945. It now produces four- and six-wheel rigid-chassis and articulated aerial ladder models as well as all-wheel drive airport crash tenders. In addition to custom vehicles American LaFrance also builds fire appliances on commercial chassis and is the largest producer of its type in the USA with over 800 employees.

Century 100′ Ladder Chief is available with Cummins or Detroit diesels of 216 to 380 bhp and various transmission options. The steel cab seats five and the bodywork is largely of aluminium. Other versions have snorkel attached to side of ladder and 300 to 1000 gpm pump.

11

AM GENERAL

AM General Corp
14250 Plymouth Road
Detroit
Michigan 48232
USA

AM General is the new name (since 1971) for American Motors, special vehicle division, which itself was an amalgamation of several once-famous motor manufacturers. In 1970 it acquired the makers of the Jeep, who, as well as making off-road vehicles, supply large quantities of vans to the US Mail. In 1964 the Studebaker factory in South Bend was acquired and since then it has produced over 215,000 2½-ton and 5-ton 6×6 trucks for the US Army as well as 31,000 1¼-ton 4×4s. Even larger military trucks are produced for AM General by CCC. As well as Jeeps, postal vehicles, military trucks and trolley buses AM General makes front-wheel drive Pow-R-Paks for building into special vehicles of up to 44,000 lbs GVW.

M44A2 Series 6×6 military truck has go-anywhere payload capacity of 2½ tons and a Continental multi-fuel engine of undisclosed output. It has replaced the GMC 2½-tonner as the American Army's standard medium-weight truck.

12

Jeep Honcho made by American Motors is for pay-loads of up to 1875 kg and has six-cylinder, 4.2-litre (258 cu ins), or V-8, 5.9-litre (360 cu ins), petrol engines and four-speed synchromesh or automatic gearboxes.

Typical of vehicles produced for the US Mail which come in ½- and 1-ton capacities is the **FJ-8** and 9 with the same engine choices as the Honcho. Three-speed automatic transmission is standard.

13

ANT

BTB Engineering Ltd
Davyfield Road
Roman Road Industrial Estate
Blackburn BB1 2NB
England

Reliant sold the production and sales rights of their TW9 vehicle to BTB in May 1978 but continue to make the engine gearbox and back axle for the revised TW9 known as the Ant, and also produce complete lighter commercial vehicles (outside the scope of this book). Roughly half of the Ant's 500 annual output is exported and it is produced as an 812 kg (16 cwt) capacity three-wheeler for a number of specialist purposes or as a 1428 kg (28 cwt) artic.

Ant **Box Artic** has 12.2 cu m alloy body. The cab is of fibreglass and the Reliant 850 cc petrol engine and four-speed gearbox give 35 to 40 mpg. Other types of trailer are produced as well as a wide choice of bodywork for the rigid chassis.

ASTRA

Astra SpA
Via Caorsana 79
1–29100 Piacenza
Italy

Founded in 1946 to recondition military vehicles, Astra made its first dumptruck in 1955. It now produces crane-carrier chassis, on- and off-road military and civilian vehicles, and dumptrucks of up to 38,000 kg capacity with Fiat, Mercedes-Benz and Detroit diesels. Most have steel half-cabs but a recent development has been a full width fibreglass design which can be tilted for access. Astras are currently exported to over thirty countries.

BM 25 M 6×4 artic (right) for up to 65,000 kg GCW. It can have a 17,174 cc Fiat V-8 diesel developing 259 kW (352 bhp) or a Mercedes-Benz 15,950 cc, V-10 developing 236 kW (320 bhp). Five-speed Allison automatic or nine-speed ZF manual gearboxes are available. Rigid chassis payload is 28,000 kg and the tilt cab is of fibreglass. On the left is an Astra **BM 20** with Mercedes-Benz 11,580 cc, six-cylinder diesel of 195 kW (265 bhp) output. It has 6×6 and a two-range, six-speed manual gearbox.

15

AUTOCAR

Autocar Trucks Division of
  White Motor Corporation
PO Box 91500
Cleveland
Ohio 44101
USA

Autocar made cars and motor tricycles from 1897, but from 1907 gradually concentrated on a 1.5-ton, two-cylinder-engined truck (with driver sitting over engine) which stayed in production until 1920. Thereafter they specialized in heavier hand-made vehicles and in 1953 were acquired by the White Motor Company, and now make approximately 2000 custom-built trucks per year for on- and off-road haulage. They are normal-control (conventional, in American parlance) vehicles using various engines, usually Cummins or Caterpillar, and bolted chassis.

Constructktor 2 range covers 2- and 3-axle models with GVW of 48,000 to 75,000 lbs. Diesels of 210 to 430 bhp are available. Ultra-heavy model has double chassis section.

AVELING-BARFORD

Aveling Barford Ltd
Invicta Works
Grantham
Lincolnshire
England

Once famous for their steam-rollers, Aveling-Barford, whose forerunners built the first successful model in 1867, continue to make road-building, quarrying and civil engineering vehicles, including a wide range of dumptrucks. They are members of the British Leyland Motor Corporation Special Products Division.

Centaur 50 has V-16 Detroit 635 bhp diesel and torque converter powershift transmission providing six forward gears. It has Nitroleo suspension (nitrogen/oil filled rams) and is for loads of 45,360 kg (100,000 lbs). Other models start at 15,422 kg (34,000 lbs) capacity.

17

AVTOEXPORT

Avtoexport
14, U1. Volkhonka
119902 Moscow G-19
USSR

The early Russian commercial vehicle industry disappeared with the Revolution to be replaced by factories each producing particular types of vehicle in the thirties. The names or initials of the factory or location were applied to their products, e.g. Gorki Auto Works—Gaz; Minsk Auto Works—Maz; and Likhachev Works in Moscow—Zil. Vehicles that are sold outside Russia are handled by Avtoexport and to simplify marketing are often called Belaz whatever their factory of origin. The true Belaz models are 30–75-ton capacity dumptrucks. The following selection of models are shown with their original names. Many of the designs were becoming antiquated by 1978 when a new Kamaz range appeared using Western technology. Ford did some of the original preparation for production and Renault helped to plan the factory. Total Russian truck production in 1980 is estimated at 800,000, of which 150,000 will be Kamaz.

The tilt-cab **Kamaz** range uses a new V-8 10,850 cc diesel developing 162 kW (220 bhp). It has a five speed, synchro gearbox, 6×4 with double reduction axles and a GVW of 22,360 kg.

UAZ 4×4 vehicles are sold in Britain as Trekmasters, though they are also produced with 4×2. The example shown, a **452D**, is for 1.075-ton loads and has a four-cylinder, 80 bhp, petrol engine and two-range, four-speed gearbox.

Modelled on World War II US Army designs the **Kraz** 3-axle range have V-8 14,866 cc, 265 gross bhp diesels and two-range, five-speed gearboxes (synchro on top four ratios). Power-assisted steering is fitted and 6×4 and 6×6 versions for up to 60 tons GCW are available. The 256 model is sold in Britain as the Belaz 15-ton dumptruck.

BEDFORD

Vauxhall Motors Ltd
PO Box 3
Luton
Bedfordshire
England

After Vauxhall were bought by General Motors, Chevrolet trucks were built in Britain until 1931 when it was decided that the market was sufficiently important to warrant an entirely British design. The Bedford was the result and the company is now one of the largest producers and exporters of trucks in the world. The three millionth Bedford was made in 1978, of which half a million had been TK models. From 1980 Bedford sold the Isuzu 1-ton pick-up under its own name in the UK.

CF range includes 230, 250, 280 and 350, the numbers indicating, as on most larger Bedfords, the GVW in kg divided by ten. 1759 and 2279 cc petrol and 1998 cc diesel engines are available. All have four cylinders and develop respectively 50, 60 and 44 kW (67, 80.5 and 59 bhp).

TK range covers 4×2 and 6×2 models (some with twin steer) for 7.37 tons to 16 tons GVW and up to 24 tons GTW with 73 kW to 112 kW (98 to 151 bhp) diesels. Shown is a **TK 1260 (KG)** for 12.35 tons GVW with 8198 cc (500 cu ins), six-cylinder, 94.3 kW (126.5 bhp) diesel.

TL 1930 is one of a new tilt-cab range introduced in May 1980, which covers rigids of 5.7 to 16.3 tonnes and up to 24.4 tonnes GCW. They augment the TK and share many of this range's mechanical components, including the new 8.2-litre Blue Series diesel in the larger versions (developing 95 kW/128 bhp in the 19.3 tonnes GCW model shown which has a five-speed, synchromesh, overdrive gearbox).

21

TM 4-4 is an 8-tonne capacity 4×4 with tilt cab of which £40 million worth have been ordered by the British Ministry of Defence for delivery from 1980. It uses the Bedford six-cylinder 500 series engine (8198 cc).

TM 3800 plated for 38 tonnes GTW but limited to 32 tons in UK. It has the Cummins E-290 diesel developing 273 bhp or the Detroit V-8 297 bhp diesel. A larger capacity TM 4200 for 42 tonnes GTW is also available, and other TMs are available with 2 or 3 axles as artics and rigids.

BMC SANAYI

BMC Sanayi ve Ticaret AS
Gazi Bulvari 47/49
Izmir
Turkey

Austin began exporting trucks from Britain to Turkey in 1947 and by the mid fifties had captured 38% of the market. Two years before the merger of BMC and Leyland in 1968 the former company had started a Turkish assembly plant in which they held 26% of the capital and their Turkish partners 74%. Since 1966 local material content has grown from 35% by value to 77%. Over 60,000 vehicles had been produced by 1977 and production capacity is now 20,000 per year from a 2200 workforce.

BMC Sanayi make forward-control trucks using the Redline Bathgate cab and normal-control **TM 140s**, as shown here. All use 120 bhp, 6/98 Turkish-produced Leyland diesels. Four- and five-speed, synchro gearboxes are available and GVW ranges from 10,430 to 12,700 kg.

23

BOLLNÄS

Bollnäs Verkstads Aktiebolag
PO Box 61
S-821 01 Bollnäs
Sweden

Bollnäs specializes in terminal tractors which are used for transferring semi-trailers in docks and industrial sites when their normal road tractor portion has been disconnected. To accommodate different trailer sizes a hydraulically adjustable fifth-wheel coupling is fitted. An associate company makes BT fork-lift and pallet-trucks.

Several firms make similar vehicles, notably Mol, DAF, Ottawa, Reliance-Mercury and Douglas but as this is such a specialized area of truck manufacture only one or two representative examples have been selected for this edition.

PT-25 can take an imposed load of 25,000 kg on its hydraulically height adjustable fifth wheel (turntable) and can move GTWs of over 80 tons. It has a Scania, 7.8-litre, 123 kW (167 bhp) diesel, or the more powerful DS 8 turbocharged version, and Clark torque converter transmission with four-speed gearbox. The driving controls can face forwards or backwards and the cab tilts for maintenance.

BRAVIA

Bravia S.a.r.l.
Avenida Eng.° Duarte
   Pacheco 21, 5°-A
100 Lisbõa
Portugal

BRAVIA – S. A. R. L.

Bravia is associated with VM, which makes dumpers of up to 4 tonnes capacity and trailers. Bravia began by reconditioning military vehicles and as more and more new parts were incorporated they emerged as a maker in their own right in the sixties. Today they specialize in military vehicles including armoured personnel carriers and half-tracks, as well as trucks, which are also available for civilian purposes.

Leopardo is available with 4×2, 4×4 or 6×6 and can have Perkins 140 bhp diesel engines or V-8 petrol units of 210 bhp. They have five-speed, synchro (2–5) gearboxes and are for loads of up to 8 tons. The outwardly similar Pantera uses a Perkins 170 bph. V-8 diesel and is for 38,000 lbs GVW, or as a military vehicle in the NATO 6-tonne class.

25

BRIMONT

Bennes Brimont SA
Rheims S1
France

This agricultural equipment manufacturer and trailer and bodybuilder acquired the name and manufacturing rights of the Latil forestry and industrial tractor in 1974. They continue to build this unusual vehicle under the name Brimont Latil, which retains the features in use since 1922 of normal-control, four-wheel drive, four-wheel steering, and mid-mounted winch. A forward-control version of this for load carrying has been developed.

ETR 206 has a Saviem 5.5-litre, 132 bhp diesel built under MAN licence. It steers and drives on all four wheels and has a pivot behind the cab which allows the front and rear halves of the chassis to twist independently of each other, which ensures that all wheels retain equal contact with the ground. GVW is 11 tonnes and a 155 bhp version of its standard Saviem six-cylinder engine is available.

26

CAMB

Carelli SpA
Via Fossa Signora 4
Nonantola
Modena
Italy

Italy has a number of specialist firms converting standard trucks (usually Fiat) for particular purposes. Articulated low-loaders are relatively uncommon and construction machinery is frequently moved between sites on rigid trucks. Camb's speciality is trucks using Fiat engines and transmission but their own cab and special, low frame and body so that plant can be safely and easily loaded.

Camb **BF 200** has choice of Fiat engines and is for 20 tonnes GVW. Small rear wheels and tyres and limited spring travel allow a 1 m deck height. Only the middle axle is driven. Like many Italian trucks it has right-hand drive to help the driver on narrow or mountain roads.

CATERPILLAR

Caterpillar Tractor Co
Peoria
Illinois
USA

The Caterpillar Tractor Co was formed in 1925 when two tractor makers, Holt and Best, merged. Holt tractors had featured crawler, or caterpillar, tracks since 1904, hence the name.

Today Caterpillar make an extensive range of earth-moving machinery and diesel engines, the latter widely used by other truck makers. Caterpillar build dumptrucks of 31.8, 45.4 and 77 tonnes capacity with 450, 650 and 870 gross bhp diesel engines.

777 dumptruck carries 77 tonnes (85 tons) in a body of 67 cu yds (51.3 cu m) heaped capacity. Suspension is independent oil/pneumatic, brakes are drum (front) and oil-cooled disc (rear), transmission is seven-speed automatic giving up to 37 mph and the V-12 Caterpillar diesel develops 649 kW at the flywheel (870 bhp) and is of 29.3 litres (1786 cu ins) capacity.

CCC

Crane Carrier Company
1925 N. Sheridan
PO Box 51191
Tulsa
Oklahoma 74151
USA

This Company's roots go back to 1946 when its founders started to convert ex-WD vehicles to carry cranes. In 1953 they introduced their own models for this purpose and have subsequently built special-purpose trucks for a variety of uses. These include log loaders, concrete mixer chassis, garbage trucks and oil-field vehicles as well as highway models. Most American proprietary engines are available.

Centurion Low Entry model is principally for garbage collection bodywork. It has a dropped section between its front and rear axles and its cab floor is only 18 in from the ground. Some versions have duplicated driving controls on both sides of the cab. Transmission is normally automatic and the engine (usually 230 bhp) is mounted behind the cab.

CHEVROLET

Chevrolet Motor Division,
General Motors Corporation
30007 Van Dyke Avenue
Warren, Michigan 48090
USA

Founded in 1911 by W. C. Durant, formerly of GMC, and racing driver Louis Chevrolet, the firm began to offer commercial vehicles during World War I. It became part of GMC in 1917 and during the twenties developed heavier truck models which were popular in Europe, where their successors are made under the Opel and Bedford names. Nowadays in the USA both GMC and Chevrolet market similar vehicles under their respective brand names. Since 1971 GMC has distributed Isuzu vehicles in several countries and some lighter Chevrolets are known as Chevy LUV in the USA.

Titan range corresponds with GMC's Astro and can have 2 or 3 axles and Detroit, Cummins or caterpillar diesels of up to 420 bhp. Six- to thirteen-speed manual or four- and five-speed Allison (a GMC company) automatic transmissions are available and GCW is up to 80,000 lbs. The tilt cab is of aluminium construction with fibreglass doors.

Bruin range corresponds with GMC's Brigadier and includes 2- and 3-axle rigids and tractors for up to 80,000 lbs GCW with six-wheeler and 60,000 lbs with four-wheeler. A 427 cu ins V-8 petrol engine or various diesels by Detroit, Cummins and Caterpillar are offered with numerous manual and automatic transmission options.

W70 steel tilt-cab model is for 32,600 lbs GVW and can have V-8 petrol engines of 160, 190 or 210 bhp output. The standard gearbox is a five-speed manual but other automatic and manuals are available as is a two-speed rear axle.

CHINA

China National Machinery Corp
Erh Li Kou
Hsi Chiao
Peking

With vast internal requirements for goods vehicles, China has built simple, basic trucks owing much to American designs of World War II. Their more specialized requirements have usually been met by truck imports (often French) but now they are beginning to import Western technology as well for new models to appear in the later eighties. Their current vehicles are produced in numerous state-run factories each specializing in one particular model, and usually named after the region or such general terms as Liberation, Leap Forward and Satellite.

NJ series 4-ton truck has an 80 bhp, six-cylinder petrol engine and all-steel, normal-control cab. 4 × 4 and 4 × 2 versions are produced.

CHUTING STAR

CHUTING ☆
STAR

Forward Inc
West Highway 14
Huron
South Dakota 57350
USA

Specializing in 6×6 chassis for the front discharge of
concrete, Forward claims the lowest centre of gravity
truck for maximum on-site safety. The first Chuting Star
was made in 1976 and today's models can carry 9/
11 cu yds of concrete and deliver it anywhere within
25 ft of the front axle. Extra raisable axles can be fitted
to reduce ground pressure.

Chuting Star **6 × 6** has low-profile, central cab and choice
of rear-mounted Cummins and Detroit diesels of 238
to 335 bhp with Allison automatic transmission. Front
axle capacity is 20,000 lbs and tandem axle capacity
40,000 lbs. Front-wheel drive can be disengaged.

33

CITROËN

SA Automobiles Citroën
117–167 Quai André Citroën
75747 Paris Cedex 15
France

André Citroën brought American mass-production methods to France when he introduced the first car to bear his name in 1919. It was followed by light vans and trucks and increasingly heavy vehicles, including ones with diesel engines from 1936. Citroën made heavy vehicles until 1971 but in the latter years concentrated most of its commercial vehicle efforts on its Berliet division. This was sold to Saviem/Renault in 1974 when Citroën became a division of Peugeot. In 1978 Peugeot-Citroën acquired Chrysler's European operation.

In addition to their modern-looking C35 van and chassis range for up to 1965 kg loads, Citroën still produces the **1000/1600** models, as shown here. These are for 1020 to 1675 kg loads and have 1628 or 1911 cc petrol or 1946 cc diesel engines with three-speed gearboxes and all-round torsion bar suspension. Models of similar appearance have been made since 1947.

CLINE

T & J Industries Inc
PO Box 8620
13850 Wyandotte
Kansas City
Missouri 64114
USA

Founded in 1952 to make special-purpose vehicles,
much of Cline's production today is of dumptrucks. For
a time in the seventies its trucks were sold under the
name Isco but this stopped in 1978, when the firm came
under its present ownership. Cummins-engined 25 to
65 tons capacity dumptrucks are made, which are particularly popular in 45-ton 6×4 form for opencast coal
mining. Another regular production is vehicles for use
on and off rails.

Cline **Re-Railer** is an unusual type of vehicle able to
run on or off rails to reach derailments. It has been in
production since the sixties. A 4×4 version is also produced for hauling trailers and railcars around goods
yards and this has Ford gas or Detroit diesel engines
of around 145 bhp. Drive to the rails is via the rubber
tyres.

COUNTY

County Commercial Cars Ltd
Fleet
Aldershot
Hants GU13 9RW
England

Founded in 1929, County soon became well known for their conversions to Ford trucks, usually from four- to six-wheelers. In 1948 they began to make agricultural tractors, which in 1954 became well known for their equal-size-wheel, 4×4 layout. The latest forward-control, 4×4 model is widely used for both agricultural and industrial purposes. It can handle direct loads of 16,000 lbs or else tow articulated or drawbar trailers.

FC 1174 4×4 has modular cab and Ford six-cylinder, 6578 cc (410 cu ins), 84 kW (112 bhp) diesel engine, mounted largely behind the cab in the centre of the frame (box to right of cab is for tools and equipment). There are sixteen forward and four reverse gears giving up to 36 km/h (22 mph) in high top and 2.5 km/h (1.5 mph) at maximum revs in low bottom.

36

CROWN FIRECOACH

Crown Firecoach Division of
    Crown Coach Corp
2428 East 12th Street
Los Angeles
California 90021
USA

Founded in 1904, Crown has made a wide variety of
passenger chassis as well as X-Ray vans, bullion cars,
mobile cinemas and ambulances. As a spin-off from this
work it became involved in Firecoaches for a wide
variety of fire-fighting requirements. It makes 2- and 3-
axle versions including Snorkels and Tele-Squirts for dis-
charging up to 1000 gpm at up to 85 ft. Articulated fire
escapes of up to 100 ft are available. An interesting construction feature is chassis rails with the top flange fac-
ing outwards and the bottom one inwards, which is
claimed to impart extra strength without a weight
penalty. Spring shackles can be adjusted quickly to keep
the chassis level if unevenly loaded or parked on rough
ground.

Crown Firecoach with Waterous pump, Timken axles,
Ross power steering, Spicer, Fuller or Allison transmission and choice of mid-mounted engines by Ford, Cummins, Detroit or International. A duplicated air-brake
system is fitted for additional safety.

CVS

SpA Costruzione Veicoli Speciali
29010 Roveleto
Piacenza
Italy

CVS was founded in 1975 when a number of employees broke away from Astra to start their own firm. It began by specializing in crane-carrier chassis and its range of these now includes 3-, 4-, 5- and 6-axle versions for truck-mounted crane manufacturers in Italy, France and Germany. Diesel engines are usually made by Fiat, who also supplied the V-8 unit in a new development for 1979, a front discharge 10 cu m transit concrete-mixer chassis.

CVS **FP 1040** mixer chassis has six-speed gearbox plus torque convertor and 17,174 cc Fiat V-8 diesel developing 352 bhp. Top speed is 80 km/h and the front and back axles steer. Suspension is by air and rubber and the centre two axles are driven.

DAF

DAF BV
Postbus 1055
Geldropseweg 303
Netherlands

The Van Doorne brothers became truck manufacturers in 1949, using Leyland technology for some years. In 1972 International Harvester and the Dutch government each took a one-third stake in the firm, while Volvo bought DAF's car division. DAF became members of the Club of Four (with Magirus, Saviem and Volvo) to develop new medium-weight trucks and in 1978 DAF's total production was 11,300, which included trucks, buses, terminal tractors and military vehicles.

Since 1978 DAF has made a backbone chassis truck with low sides for the distribution trade and since 1979 its heavy vehicles have been sold in South Africa under the International name with Cummins 14-litre diesels. Also in 1979 DAF announced technical links with Dodge in Britain.

2300 models have 2, 3 or 4 axles and turbocharged, 8.25-litre diesels developing 155 kW (209 bhp) or 169 kW (230 bhp) with intercooling. Six-, nine- and twelve-speed gearboxes are available and drive axles have hub reduction. Shown is a 30-ton **FAD 2305 DHU** 8 × 4 tipper.

2100 range covers 4 × 2 and 6 × 2 models for up to 32 tons GTW. They have six-cylinder, 8.25-litre diesels developing 116.5 kW (156 bhp) or 150 kW (202 bhp) when turbocharged. Six-speed, synchro or constant-mesh boxes with optional splitter are available. All have steel tilt cabs.

2800 series includes 4 × 2 and 6 × 4 models for up to 108 tons GTW. They have 11.6-litre, six-cylinder DAF engines developing 185 kW (248 bhp) when turbo-charged of 229 kW (307 bhp) when additionally charge cooled. Six-, twelve- or thirteen-speed gearboxes are available.

40

DART

Dart Truck Co
1301 Chouteau Trafficway
PO Box 321, Kansas City
Missouri 64141
USA

Founded in 1903, Dart originally made small, general-purpose trucks. In 1925 its original owner died and the firm was taken over by its chief salesman, Max W. Cline, who concentrated production on trucks for the construction and quarrying industries. In 1958 Dart was bought by Pacific Car and Foundry (Paccar) and merged with Kenworth to create KW-Dart. In 1970 it regained its old name, though still a member of the Paccar group, and now makes dumptrucks of 100 tons and upwards capacity. Unlike most vehicles of this size, which have diesel-electric drive, Dart uses conventional truck technology and standard Allison automatic transmissions, and some 300 have been sold since introduced in 1965.

Dart **3120** is largest of range and carries 120 tons (108.9 tonnes). Its heaped capacity is 90 cu yds (68.8 cu m). Suspension is by rubber and various Detroit and Cummins twelve-cylinder diesels of 1000 to 1200 bhp are available. Six-speed automatic transmission drives to a triple reduction rear axle.

41

DENNIS

Dennis Motors Ltd
Guildford
Surrey GU2 5XP
England

One of the earliest British firms to concentrate on petrol-driven commercial vehicles, Dennis started as bicycle makers and after turning to cars produced their first trucks in 1904. They have always made a wide range of trucks but in recent times have concentrated on fire-engines and municipal vehicles. After many years out of the bus field they announced a new PSV range in 1977. Various engines are used by Dennis, including Gardner, Rolls-Royce, Perkins, Ford and Leyland.

Municipal chassis with Bulkmaster compression refuse body and new Ogle-styled steel cab also found on RS fire appliance and Delta goods models. Available with various engine/transmission options but normally the Perkins 6.354 and five-speed manual gearbox.

DENNISON

Dennison Truck Manufacturing Ltd
Black Church
Rathcoole
Dublin
Ireland

George Dennison built up his own trailer company which he sold to Fruehauf. Then in 1977 he launched his own brand of truck embodying various British proprietary components. In 1979 Dennison began to use Sisu cabs and today produces a range of 2-, 3- and 4-axle vehicles all powered by Gardner or Rolls-Royce engines. Production in 1980 was three to four vehicles per week.

8×4 tipper is designed for 32,522 kg GVW or 44,706 kg GTW. Rolls-Royce 220, 265, 290 and Gardner 240 bhp diesels may be specified. There is a Fuller nine-speed gearbox and Eaton rear axles with Rubery Owen non-reactive bogie. The steel Sisu cab can be tilted.

DIAMOND-REO GIANT

Osterlund Inc
PO Box 4376
Harrisburg
Pennsylvania 17111
USA

Reo and Diamond T made trucks from 1904 and 1911 respectively. White bought both firms in the late fifties and in 1960 combined their production operations, though retained the separate names until 1967. Diamond-Reo then remained as a White subsidiary until late 1971, when it was spun off to stockholders in lieu of a dividend. Under this arrangement the company existed until 1975, when it went out of business. In the subsequent sale of its assets different designs were bought by various manufacturers but the name and production rights to its conventional models were bought by Osterlund Inc, who had begun as Diamond T distributors in 1958. Current models feature Autocar cabs and various engines of 230 to 400 bhp.

Giant **C11664DB** can have Cummins NTC 230 or NTC 290 engines or the Detroit 335 bhp diesel. Transmission is by Fuller, Dana-Spicer and Rockwell-Standard. The cab is steel with a fibreglass hood (bonnet) and the chassis is of bolted construction. The example shown is suitable for 10 cu yd transit concrete mixing.

44

DINA

Diesel Nacional SA
Miguel Laurent 803
Esquina Avenida Universidad
Mexico 12 DF

Diesel Nacional is government owned and controls the Mexican Perkins engine factory. It has produced vehicles since 1957, many of the light- and medium-weight models being of International origin (though IHC's licencee in Mexico is now Famsa) with Perkins engines. Heavier International Loadstar derived models are Cummins powered as is Dina's 861 range. Vehicles of up to 3 tons capacity are produced in a former Borgward plant and the firm is Mexico's largest maker of trucks and buses.

861 models are available as rigids or artics and have Dina-built Cummins 14-litre (855 cu ins), 261 kW (350 bhp), six-cylinder diesels and Spicer fourteen-speed (plus four reverse) gearboxes. Axles are by Rockwell. Vehicle shown with drilling rig is for a GVW of 25,401 kg (56,000 lbs).

DJB

DJB Engineering Ltd
Peterlee
County Durham SR8 2HX
England

In production since 1974, over 1000 DJB dumptrucks, logging vehicles, pipe carriers and general off-road load carriers had been made by the end of the decade. All are based on Caterpillar mechanical components and are for payloads of 22 to 55 tons.

D550 is for loads of 50 tonnes (55 tons) and has an eight-cylinder, 18-litre Caterpillar diesel developing 328 kW (450 bhp). Drive is to the middle and front axles and the vehicle has articulated frame steering. Caterpillar powershift transmission gives four gears both forwards and backwards.

DODGE

Talbot Motor Co Ltd
Boscombe Road
Dunstable
Bedfordshire LU5 4LX
England

Dodge

A branch of the American Dodge firm was established in London in the twenties and after its acquisition by Chrysler, assembly of Dodge trucks was started at Kew in 1933. After a few years Kew Dodges became wholly British in content. In 1964 Chrysler acquired a stake in the Rootes Group, who controlled the Commer and Karrier commercial vehicle firms (founded in 1905 and 1907 respectively), and in 1973 Rootes became a wholly owned subsidiary of Chrysler. In 1976 the Commer name was discontinued and replaced by Dodge, who also renamed Barreiros and Simca commercial vehicles sold in Britain. The Karrier name ended in 1979. In 1978 PSA Peugeot-Citroën acquired all of Chrysler's European operation and renamed it Talbot. The heaviest Dodge models sold in Britain, the 300 series, are produced in Spain.

Spacevan comes in 914 and 1118 kg (18 and 22 cwt) capacities and can have Talbot 1.72-litre petrol or Perkins 1.75-litre diesel engines and four-speed, synchro gearbox (plus overdrive on some models). Over 15,000 are operated by the GPO.

Dodge 50 Series, new in 1979, uses some styling features from US Chrysler Dodges and covers five basic models from 3.5 (shown here) to 7.5 tonnes GVW. Engines include Talbot 1981 cc or Dodge 3685 cc petrol or Perkins 4.236 or 6.247 diesels. Automatic or manual transmission is available, as are factory-built vans of 9.4 or 12.8 cu m (335 or 450 cu ft).

Commando 100 Series includes twelve basic models from the **GO8** shown here for 7.5 tonnes GVW up to 16.26 tonnes GVW and 26.40 tonnes GTW. Most have Perkins six-cylinder engines though in some of the heaviest models Perkins V-8 or Mercedes-Benz diesels are offered. Cabs tilt and four-, five- or six-speed manual or Allison automatic transmissions are fitted.

DODGE

Chrysler Corp
PO Box 1919
Detroit
Michigan 48288
USA

Dodge began making cars in 1914, afterwards diversifying into light commercials and buses. Since 1928 they have been members of the Chrysler Corporation and over the years have made progressively heavier vehicles, though with growing financial difficulties in the seventies they have returned to light vehicles—their largest model being an 18,000 lb GVW motor-home chassis using a 7.3-litre engine produced by International Harvester. In 1978 they sold their British, French and Spanish subsidiaries to PSA Peugeot-Citroen who continue to make commercial vehicles under the Dodge name. A number of US Dodge's lighter pick-ups are made for them by Mitsubishi, who also produce small diesels for them and in certain export markets, notably Australia, some Mitsubishi heavy trucks are sold as Dodge Fusos. Some Dodge models in America are available with the Plymouth division of Chrysler's name.

Dodge **B200** van has a GVW of 6400 lbs (2903 kg) and can have 3.7-, 5.2- or 5.9-litre petrol engines (225, 318 or 360 cu ins). A four-speed manual overdrive gearbox or three-speed automatic is available.

DODGE

Automoviles Talbot
Apartado 140
Madrid—14
Spain

CAMIONES

In 1951 Eduardo Barreiros began to make diesel conversions for petrol engines. From these developed a range of diesels, which in 1958 were fitted in the first Barreiros trucks. Between 1961 and 1974 the British firm AEC had commercial and technical links with Barreiros, but from 1963 Chrysler began buying into the firm and by 1967 had a 77% stake and had changed its name to Chrysler España SA. In 1978 the Barreiros name was dropped from its trucks in Spain and they became Dodges (under which name they had been sold in other parts of Europe for some time). In late 1978 PSA Peugeot-Citroën acquired Chrysler's European holdings including the Spanish company.

Amongst a range of 2-, 3- and 4-axle rigid Dodges all sharing the same basic tilt cab is this **C-38** for 38 tonnes GTW. It has a Dodge 11,946 cc, six-cylinder diesel developing 275 bhp and an eight-speed, synchromesh gearbox. The smallest model is a 5320 cc, 120 bhp engined, 14,000 kg GVW truck, whilst the largest tractors have a turbocharged version of the C-38 engine developing 320 bhp or alternatively the Cummins E350.

DOUGLAS

F. L. Douglas (Equipment) Ltd
Village Road
Arle
Cheltenham
England

In 1947 Douglas began by converting AEC Matadors for timber extraction and quickly developed its own range of special-purpose vehicles. These included off-road lorries, fire appliances, crane-carriers, snow ploughs, dumptrucks, container handlers and, from the mid fifties, special aircraft tugs and elevating fifth wheel terminal tractors named Tugmasters. Since the early sixties Douglas has concentrated on tugs of all sorts which are to be seen at docks and airports around the world. Over fifty airlines buy Tugmasters, and these and trailer tugs come in a wide range of sizes with engines by Perkins, Bedford, Leyland and Caterpillar.

Tugmaster NS8 250 has a Leyland six-cylinder, 250 bhp diesel, torque converter transmission, two-way driving controls, and can handle any semi-trailer up to 65 tons that comes ashore from a ferry. Note the elevating coupling to suit different trailers.

51

DUPLEX

Warner and Swasey Co
Winona
Minnesota
USA

Starting as the Dolson Automobile Co. in 1904 and changing its name to Duplex in 1909, this company specialized in 4×4 trucks from an early stage. In 1955 it became part of the Warner and Swasey group and specialized in crane-carriers, fire appliance chassis, snow-plough and road-maintenance trucks. Most of its fire chassis are built to the order of FMC Corp, Dearborn Street, Tipton, Indiana 46072, who sell them fully equipped under their own name or that of their subsidiary, Bean. In 1977 Duplex became independent once again and announced that it would move to Ohio.

Duplex fire chassis are available with various engines. This **R-300** ladder truck has a V-8 Detroit diesel and automatic transmission. It is equipped with a 1250 gpm pump and Bean bodywork and equipment.

EBRO

Motor Iberica SA
Avda Capital Lopez Varela 149
Apartado 680
Barcelona 5
Spain

Founded in 1920 to produce Fords in Spain, the company became Spanish owned in 1954 and its name was
changed from Ford Motor Iberica to Motor Iberica. It
produced trucks based on British Ford Thames under
the name of a major Spanish river, the Ebro, and in 1971
acquired the makers of Siata and Avia commercial
vehicles. In 1966 Motor Iberica joined forces with Perkins and Massey-Ferguson in Spain, and is involved
with the production and distribution of Jeeps in Spain.
Ebro makes 25,000 trucks, 20,000 vans, 125,000
engines and 35,000 farm tractors per year. In 1980 Nissan purchased a 36% stake in the firm.

F-275 has the Perkins 4.108, 1760 cc, 36.8 kW
(50 bhp), four-cylinder diesel and four-speed, synchro
gearbox. It comes with a choice of van and truck bodywork and, in the form shown, carries 1200 kg. It has a
beam front axle and British clutch and prop shaft.

Tilt-cab E range includes 4×2 models for loads of 1580 kg to 8200 kg with Perkins four- and six-cylinder diesels. Unusual versions include a backbone chassis model to give low side-loading and the 4×4 **E-70/1** shown here. This has a 76 bhp, Ebro-produced, Perkins four-cylinder diesel and five-speed gearbox with two-speed transfer box. Payload is 3700 kg.

The heavyweight P range includes 2- and 3-axle trucks and tractors with Perkins 6.354 or V-8 540 diesels. GTW is from 13,700 kg to 27,000 kg and GVW from 9440 kg on **P-137** model shown here to 22,000 kg. Five- or six-speed gearboxes are fitted and a two-speed axle is available. The cab tilts.

ERF

ERF Ltd
Sun Works
Sandbach
Cheshire CW11 9DN
England

Edwin Richard Foden built the first diesel lorry bearing his initials in 1933. Over the years the company has carved out an important niche in the British maximum gross vehicle weight category (17% of rigid 4-axle UK market in 1979 and 15% of 4×2 tractive units) and today produces 2-, 3- and 4-axle heavy trucks. The new B series 4×2, 6×2 and 6×4 models introduced in 1974 feature a steel-framed cab panelled in hot-pressed SMC which meets proposed EEC safety standards.

M series 16-ton GVW truck has choice of Dorman V-8 or Gardner 6LXB diesels each developing approximately 160 bhp. It has a five-speed gearbox, power steering, tilt cab and a frame height of only 923 mm to suit the distribution trades.

B series eight-wheelers are available with Gardner, Rolls-Royce or Cummins diesels of up to 260 bhp installed output. Six- or nine-speed gearboxes are available and the example shown is operating at 30 tons GVW. The B series also covers 2- and 3-axle models.

Heavy-duty, sleeper-cab tractor built to Middle Eastern specification with air conditioning and Cummins 335 or Rolls-Royce 290 bhp diesels. Similar vehicles are supplied to South Africa and sold through Leyland's distributor network.

EUCLID

Euclid Inc
22221 St Clair Avenue
Cleveland
Ohio 44117
USA

Founded in 1926 as a division of a crane maker, Euclid
became a separate company in 1931 and began to produce dumptrucks in 1933. In 1953 General Motors
acquired the company, but in 1968 sold it to White, who
added assembly plants in Belgium, Australia, South
Africa and Canada. Meanwhile General Motors introduced their own competing Terex dumptrucks. In
1977 White sold their Euclid subsidiary to Mercedes-
Benz' controlling company, Daimler-Benz AG.

R-100 from a range of rear dumps of 25 to 170 tons
capacity is for 90,720 kg (100-ton) loads and has Cummins or Detroit engines of 1050 and 1000 gross bhp.
Allison six-speed automatic transmission provides up to
40.6 mph and suspension is by trailing arms and rubber
elements. Heaped body capacity is 76.6 cu yds.

57

FABCO

Kelsey-Hayes Company
Fabco Div
1249 67th Street
Oakland
California 94608
USA

Kelsey-Hayes is a subsidiary of the Fruehauf Corporation. Its main business is front-drive axles and transfer boxes for the heavy truck industry or for converting existing trucks. However, it also produces small quantities of specialist vehicles like yard spotters and all-wheel drive trucks for collecting produce from the fields and delivering it direct to market without trans-shipment. The latter are popular in the California lettuce fields, where they are built to a special track width to suit the plant rows and have 6 × 6 to enable them to traverse recently irrigated soil. Auxiliary gearboxes enable these trucks to travel at less than 1 mph in the fields and 55 mph towing a trailer on the way to market, which is normally within 60 miles.

Widetrack **Field Harvester** has Detroit 4-53 turbo-charged diesel, Clark five-speed gearbox with Dana three-speed auxiliary and Fabco two-speed transfer box. It has 6 × 6 with all axles produced by Fabco and a GVW of 30,000 lbs.

58

FAP

FAP FAMOS
11 Oktomvri Autokaroserija
Francuska 61
Beograd
Yugoslavia

FAP is Yugoslavia's best-known engine maker, supplying vehicle manufacturers in several neighbouring countries. It began to produce commercial vehicles in 1953 (often based on Saurer designs) and now makes four- and six-wheel, medium and heavy-duty trucks and PSVs, which all contain a high proportion of FAP's own components.

The **1516/80** rigid 4×2, shown here with refrigerated van bodywork, has a six-cylinder, 8280 cc diesel developing 107 kW (145 bhp) and a five forward-speed gearbox.

FAUN

Faun-Werke
Zentralverwaltung
8560 Lauf an der Pegnitz
PO Box 8
West Germany

An engineering firm dating from 1845, they built a steam-driven fire-engine in 1890 and concentrated on municipal and special-purpose vehicles thereafter. A petrol-electric 10-tonner was built in 1908 followed by ambulances in World War I. In 1918 the company first used the name Faun, taking the first letters of their title Fahrzeugwerke Ansbach und Nürnberg. In 1921 they made double-decker buses for Berlin. Through the twenties and thirties they concentrated on municipal vehicles, which still form an important part of their business, along with fire-fighting vehicles, crane-carriers with up to 8 axles, dumptrucks, and heavy-haulage tractors.

Faun make dumptrucks for loads of 18 to 85 tons with engines of 141 to 597 kW (192 to 811 bhp) by Cummins and Detroit. This is the **K 85.8,** the largest in their range, with powershift transmission and 52.5 cu m heaped body capacity.

Crane-carrier chassis produced by Faun include 3-, 4-, 5-, 6-, 7- and 8-axle machines for cranes of 25 to 500 tons. Engines are usually by Deutz or MTU and range in output from 141 kW (192 bhp) to 390 kW (530 bhp). Shown is a **KF 125.63/64** model for 125-ton cranes which has a 282 kW (384 bhp) diesel and steering on all but the two driving axles.

Faun make a wide assortment of heavy-haulage tractors with 4×4, 6×6, 8×6 and 8×8 drive, forward- or normal-control, and various makes of diesel ranging from 184 kW (250 bhp) to 574 kW (780 bhp). They have six, eight or fifteen forward gears and the largest can tow over 300 tons. Shown is an **HZ 36.40/45** with Deutz 268 kW (365 bhp) air-cooled diesel.

FBW

FBW Fahrzeug AG
Motorenstrasse 100
Wetzikon 4
Switzerland CH-8621

Franz Brozincevic made his first truck in 1910 under the name Franz and from 1911 was one of the first continental manufacturers to specify only shaft instead of chain drive on his vehicles. From 1918 they were known as FBW, the W standing for the town where they were made. In 1924 the first Henschel vehicles were FBWs built under licence in Germany. In 1949 FBW introduced underfloor-engined buses and trucks and today similar vehicles are made plus normal-control tippers and heavy-haulage tractors, off-road vehicles, articulated trolley-buses and diesel engines of 130 to 260 bhp. Vehicle output amounts to about 150 per year. In 1978 FBW was taken over by the Swiss industrial group of Oerlikon Buhrle.

4×4 fire appliance has six-cylinder, 206 kW (280 bhp), FBW 11.95-litre diesel and Allison three- to six-speed automatic transmission or eight-speed, ZF synchro gearbox. Rear axle has double reduction and front, hub reduction.

A horizontal version of FBW's 11.95-litre diesel is used in passenger vehicles and certain haulage models, like this refuse collector. The same transmission options are available as on the fire appliance or FBW's own five-speed splitter gearbox.

6×6 tipper has turbocharged version of 11.95-litre diesel developing 235 kW (320 bhp) and same transmission options as above. Like all FBWs it has a hydraulic retarder built into the gearbox to save the brakes on long mountain descents.

FIAT

Fiat Veicoli Industriali SpA
Via Puglia 35
CP 1371
10100 Torino
Italy

Fiat was founded in 1899 and made its first truck in 1903 and bus in 1906. It has bought various other commercial vehicle makers over the years, including OM in 1938, Lancia and Unic in 1969 (which belonged to Simca from 1952 and which acquired the French Saurer factory in 1956). Fiat also has close ties with Alfa-Romeo, who, with Saviem, have a joint van factory in Spain and a joint diesel engine company (Sofim) in Italy. In 1975 KHD, the makers of Magirus-Deutz, and Fiat jointly formed IVECO (Industrial Vehicles Corporation) which is now wholly Fiat controlled. Fiat trucks are built under licence in some twenty countries.

Daily range (Grinta when OM) covers 3–4 tonnes GVW. Shown is a crew-cab version with Sofim four-cylinder, 2445 cc, 53 kW diesel and four-speed, synchro gearbox (five speeds optional). Front suspension is independent by torsion bars. Cab shown seats seven, but a deeper version seats nine.

Produced by Lancia with either Fiat, OM or OM-Saurer badges is the 65, 75 and 90PC range of 4×4s for GVW of 7000, 7850 and 9800 kg respectively. The smallest has a four-cylinder, 3666 cc, 62.5 kW (85 bhp) diesel and the larger models (**75PC** shown here) have six-cylinder, 5184 cc, 90 kW (122 bhp) diesels. All have a two-range, five-speed gearbox and the 65 and 75 can have infinitely variable hydrostatic transmission for such duties as snow clearance.

Z range covers ten models for payloads of 2600 to 6800 kg. Three diesels (two of four cylinders, one of six) are available, depending on GVW, of 62.6, 73.6 and 95.7 kW (85, 100 or 130 bhp). Gearbox has five speeds (synchro on top four). A tilt cab is optional on models above 8 tonnes GVW.

The same basic tilt-cab structure is now used on several Fiat medium and heavy models as well as by OM, Unic and Magirus Deutz. This is the **330.35** 6×4 tipper for 33 tonnes GVW or up to 56 tonnes GTW. It has a 17,174 cc Fiat V-8 diesel developing 259 kW (352 bhp) and eight-speed, synchro gearbox with or without torque converter.

A large range of medium to heavy models use the earlier fixed cab shown on this **697N** 6×4 rigid in use as a heavy-haulage tractor. It has a 13,798 cc, 260 bhp, six-cylinder diesel and eight-speed, synchro gearbox. GVW is up to 26,500 kg (58,406 lbs) and with suitable reduction axles a GTW of 156,000 kg (343,800 lbs) is attainable.

FLEXTRUCK

Flextruck Limited
PO Box 250
Breslau
Ontario N0B 1M0
Canada

Under the name Rubber Railways, around 100 ingenious chassis for transit mixers were made up to 1976. The company ownership then changed but the basic design continued under the control of Care Equipment's Rubber Railroads. The name is now Flextruck and the design consists of an articulated frame for carrying front-discharge concrete mixers of up to 11 cu yds capacity. The rear-mounted engine drives the front three rigid axles whilst the others trail and the hindmost can be raised for unladen travel.

MF511 6×10 chassis has 20 degree pivot steering, rear-mounted Detroit V-8 305 bhp diesel and Spicer six-speed gearbox. Unladen weight is 26,000 lbs and GVW with laden mixer is 98,000 lbs. Overall length is 36 ft and both driving and mixing controls are in the one-man cab.

FODEN

Fodens Ltd
Elworth Works
Sandbach
Cheshire CW11 9HZ
England

Famed for agricultural machinery in the last century, Fodens continued to use steam power for the lorries they produced from 1900 until their first diesel in 1931. They now make an extensive range of maximum-capacity road vehicles as well as off-road dumptrucks. A recent development has been on-/off-road vehicles to military specification and, for the first time in over twenty years, bus chassis. Kits for vehicle assembly overseas are also produced. In 1980 the firm was acquired by Paccar, the owner of Kenworth, Peterbilt and Dart.

S10 Haulmaster 24 tons GVW truck has Gardner 180 bhp, six-cylinder or Cummins V-8, 8.3-litre, 207 bhp diesels. In Cummins form it has a Fuller range-change, nine-speed gearbox. A combination of light-weight rubber rear suspension and steel-frame grp cab giving a wet chassis weight of only 6180 kg (6.08 tons) which allows a payload/body allowance of almost 18 tons under UK regulations.

Dockspotter is produced in South Africa from kits supplied from UK. Over 150 are in service with SA Railways. Automatic transmission is available and power is provided by Cummins NTC230 diesels.

Haulmaster 8 × 4 can have leaf-spring or rubber rear suspension and Gardner, Cummins or Rolls-Royce diesels of up to 265 bhp. It has a steel/grp tilt cab and range-change gearbox. GVW is 30 tons. A similar cab is used on the other highway models including 4 × 2 tractive units for 32–38 tons GCW with engines up to 290 bhp.

New **dumptruck** range from 1979 features 2- and 3-axle models with rubber suspension, Cummins engines of 280 to 380 bhp, Allison automatic gearboxes, I beam chassis and payloads of 18.14 to 31.75 tonnes (20 to 35 short tons).

6×6 **tractor** from range of 4×4, 6×4, 6×6 and 8×4 heavy-duty civilian and military vehicles, all of which share this pattern of steel Motor Panels cab except for a low-profile crane-carrier. They have Cummins or Rolls-Royce diesels of 220 to 400 bhp. This tractor is for 65 tonnes GTW, while others go up to 150 tonnes GTW.

FORD

Ford Motor Company Ltd
Eagle Way
Brentwood
Essex CM13 3BW
England

American-designed light trucks were assembled in Britain from 1915 with the proportion of British parts gradually increasing over the years. In the early thirties Ford moved into a purpose-built factory at Dagenham and in more recent times the truck division moved to Brentwood and Langley to allow for general expansion. In addition to the parent company in the USA, Ford produce trucks in various parts of the world, with the British operation their largest in Europe, producing an extensive range of vehicles. In 1975 they moved into the UK heavy truck market for the first time with their Dutch-built Transcontinental rigid and articulated models which use Cummins engines and basic cab structures from Berliet.

Parcel van version of the **Transit** is based on the 100 and 160 chassis/cowl for GVW of approximately 2550 kg and 3320 kg (5617/7313 lbs). Engines are 2-litre petrol or 2.4-litre diesel. Automatic transmission or overdrive are available on some Transit models.

A Series covers models of 3500 kg to 6300 kg GVW (3.442–6.2 tons) and can have 3-litre petrol and 2.4- or 3.5-litre diesel engines of up to 93 bhp. This is the **A0609** with 3.5-litre, 66.4 kW (89 bhp) diesel.

D Series starts at the **D0607** with a GVW of 5893 kg (5.8 tons) the first two model letters showing its nominal GVW and the second two showing a tenth of its net bhp. In this case the engine is the Ford four-cylinder, 4.2-litre diesel with four-speed gearbox (synchro on top three ratios).

D2418 is largest of a range of 6×2 and 6×4 tandems which cover GVW of 17,273 to 24,385 kg (17 to 24 tons). Available with a two- or four-leaf spring bogie, the D2418 and 2417 have the same engines as the D2818/17 and usually the same gearbox. The largest Ford-powered model is the D2414 with turbocharged 6-litre, six-cylinder diesel.

Transcontinental 6×4 heavy-haulage tractor for up to 44,000 kg GTW has nine- or thirteen-speed gearbox and choice of various versions of the 14-litre Cummins E Series up to 259 kW (345 bhp) in turbocharged and aftercooled form. Cab tilts and has room for two bunks.

73

FORD

The American Road
Dearborn
Michigan 48121
USA

Henry Ford built his first car in 1896 and introduced
mass-production to the motor industry with his immortal
Model T, produced in car and commercial vehicle form
from 1908 until 1927. The Model T was followed by
increasingly heavy goods models, amongst which, in the
mid thirties, were the first with V-8 engines. Ford in
America now produces light car-based commercials and
small 4×4s right up to maximum capacity road haulage
tractors.

F-Series medium duty range covers trucks of 11,113 kg
(24,500 lbs) to 14,062 kg (31,000 lbs) GVW and GCW
up to 27,216 kg (60,000 lbs). Gasoline engines are V-
8s of 6.1 litres (370 cu ins) or 7 litres (429 cu ins). Four-
speed manual or automatic and five-speed manual gearboxes are available.

L-Series covers 2- and 3-axle models from 10,886 kg (24,000 lbs) to 36,787 kg (81,100 lbs) GVW. They have Ford V-8 gasoline or Caterpillar and Cummins diesels of up to 350 bhp. L stands for Louisville, Kentucky, where this range is produced.

CL-9000 range is for up to 62,595 kg (138,000 lbs) GCW and can have Cummins, Detroit or Caterpillar diesels of up to 600 bhp. Six- to thirteen-speed transmissions are offered and the tilt cab is made from aluminium and comes with various night/day options with BBC dimensions down to 54 ins.

FREIGHTLINER

Freightliner Corp
4747 North Channel Avenue
PO Box 3849
Portland
Oregon 97208
USA

Conceived by Consolidated Freightways, a major transport firm, for its own use in 1939, Freightliners were not offered to outside operators until 1949. Two years after that White took on the nationwide marketing, which they retained until 1976. Roughly 80% of Freightliner's 15,000 annual production from factories in Canada, California, Indiana, North Carolina and Oregon is of cab-over models, which account for almost a quarter of the American total. A feature of all models since the outset has been their low tare weight. Alongside its own vehicles the company is also responsible for Volvo truck sales in North America.

6 × 4 'conventionals' (normal control) have been produced since 1974 and this the **FLC-12064T** which can have Cummins, Caterpillar, Detroit or Allis-Chalmers diesels of 290 to 650 bhp. Cab is aluminium and chassis, wheels and other components can also be in this material.

FTF

Floor's Handel en Industrie BV
Havenweg 4
Wijchen (bij Nijmegen)
Holland

Floor began by importing Mack trucks and from the mid sixties developed its own specialized trucks, initially using Mack components. It now produces about 150 vehicles per year, mainly heavy-haulage tractors and all-wheel-drive tippers. They have Detroit engines and cabs by Motor Panels Ltd of Coventry, UK.

Oilfield 6×4 is for 50 tonnes GVW and has 242 kW (324 bhp) Detroit diesel, various transmission options, including Allison automatic, and Motor Panels steel tilt cab with grp front panel.

FWD

FWD Corporation
East 12th Street
Clintonville
Wisconsin 54929
USA

In 1906 the founders of the Four Wheel Drive Auto Co designed a 4×4 light steam chassis able to operate in mud and snow impossible for 4×2 vehicles. The 4×4 was soon redesigned with a petrol engine, which in heavier form proved invaluable in the difficult operating conditions of World War I. FWD has concentrated on multi-wheel drive chassis over the years which have Tractioneer lockable differentials with torque split between the axles in proportion to load. FWD also makes fire-engines, having acquired the long-established Seagrave firm in 1963.

CB 4×4 Tractioneer for GVW up to 44,000 lbs can have aluminium cab as shown with fibreglass roof or steel cabover (forward-control) design. Various gas and diesel engines of 130 to 300 bhp are available. Five-speed manual gearboxes are standard but seven, eight, ten and twelve speeds as well as automatic transmission are available. One-, two- or three-speed transfer boxes are fitted and chassis shown is for snow clearance.

GINAF

Ginaf Automobielbedrijven BV
Bruinehorst 28 Postbus 1
Ederveen
Netherlands

Like RAM, Ginaf began by modernizing ex-military American trucks for use as heavy-duty, off-road tippers. Most of their current production is of forward-control 6×4, 6×6 and 8×8 vehicles using many DAF components, including cabs. They also continue to make bonneted 6×6 trucks of similar appearance to former US Army trucks, but using current components, 8×6 crane chassis with low-slung cabs are also made.

KFS 12 is for 14,018 kg payloads and has choice of 175 or 236 bhp DAF diesels. It has a ZF six-speed gearbox plus two-range transfer box and Rockwell axles. Other sizes of 6×6 chassis are made and there is also a long-wheelbase 6×4 model for normal road haulage with 15,500 kg payload.

GMC

General Motors Corporation
GMS Truck and Coach Div
660 South Boulevard East
Pontiac
Michigan 48053
USA

William C. Durant took control of Buick in 1903 and in 1908 formed the General Motors Company which took over several pioneer car and truck manufacturers. From 1911 the truck names were changed to GMC and Durant moved on to promote Chevrolet, which was taken over by GMC during World War I. The General Motors Truck Company, following another merger in 1925, changed its name to Yellow Truck and Coach and in 1943 GMC bought the assets of the company. It ranks first now in USA truck sales with a range of light to heavy vehicles, many of which are also sold under the Chevrolet name. GMC owns the makers of two widely used commercial vehicle components: Allison automatic transmission and Detroit diesels.

GMC 5000 and 6000 Series conventionals have traditionally had 125 to 190 bhp petrol engines but to accommodate larger diesels this revised tilt-forward fibreglass hood (bonnet) **Top Kick** version was added in 1980. Caterpillar, Detroit and Cummins diesels are to be available and 50% of the American mid-weight market is expected to be diesel powered in 1985 compared with 9.6% in 1978.

GMC Vandura models are made with 110 or 125 in wheelbases for loads of up to 4335 lbs. Shown is the **G-2500** for 6,600 lbs GVW available with straight-six or V-8 petrol engines of 4.1 to 6.6 litres and power outputs of 130 to 185 bhp. It can have three-speed manual or automatic transmissions. Like other models in the GMC range, Chevrolet versions are available.

GMC General range corresponds with the Chevrolet Bison and covers 2- and 3-axle models in rigid and tractor form. GVW on 2-axle models is 33,860 lbs and on 3-axles 44,860, whilst corresponding GTW is 80,000 lbs for both types. Various Detroit, Cummins and Caterpillar diesels of up to 420 bhp are available. Options include tyre pressure warning light, air suspension and automatic transmission. The cab is constructed from aluminium and fibreglass.

HAHN

Hahn Motors Inc
Hamburg
Pennsylvania
USA

William G. Hahn made carriages from 1898 and in 1907 produced his first motor vehicles. In 1913 the company made its first fire appliance and subsequently specialized in them. Today it makes 80 to 90 fire-engines per year on both its own and bought-in chassis. The former usually have Detroit, Cummins or Waukesha engines.

Hahn **Custom** appliances normally have Detroit 265 bhp or 350 bhp, and Cummins 295 bhp (as here) diesels or Waukesha 325 bhp gasoline engines. This example has Allison automatic transmission, Rockwell axles, 500-gallon water tank, 1000 gpm Hale pump, five-man cab and 2000 ft hose capacity.

HAULAMATIC

Haulamatic Ltd
Heanor Gate Road
Heanor
Derbyshire DE7 7SB
England

Realizing the heavy pounding that the transmission of site vehicles suffers, Haulamatic in 1961 converted a Commer to automatic transmission. By 1969 they were making their own chassis and today make 3-axle dumptrucks. These include 3-axle rigid models and, new in 1980, a 22-ton capacity pivot steer model. In 1979 Blackwood Hodge adopted its distribution in place of the Magirus Deutz dumptrucks it had handled previously.

620 Mk 11 has a Perkins V-8 215 bhp diesel and Allison five-speed automatic transmission plus the option of a Caterpillar engine. Off-road payload is 20 tonnes. The 13 cu m capacity (heaped) body is heated by exhaust gases for easy discharge. The truck has leaf springs all round, those at the rear supporting rocking beams.

HEATHFIELD

Heathfield Engineering Ltd
Shaldon Road
Newton Abbot
Devon TQ12 4SQ
England

Heathfield began producing dumptrucks in 1967. They
feature rubber suspension for simple maintenance and
their exhaust gases pass through the body walls to warm
sticky loads and make them discharge easily. 20-, 30-
and 33-tonne capacity models are produced on two
axles. In 1978 an on-/off-road 6×4 tipper was produced
which is currently undergoing evaluation. In 1979 the
firm, which is part of the Centrax engineering group,
took up production of the Nordverk pivot steer 6×6 for
its British distributor (SLD Olding of Hatfield) after the
Swedish factory had closed.

H33 dumptruck is for 30-tonne (66,000 lbs) loads. It
has 4×2, rubber suspension, five-speed Allison automatic transmission. Cummins or Caterpillar diesels of up
to 280 kW (375 bhp) gross and a heaped body capacity
of up to 26 cu yds.

HENDRICKSON

Mobile Equipment Div
Hendrickson Mfg Co
8001 West 47th Street
Lyons Illinois
USA

Hendrickson are best known in worldwide trucking for their proprietary tandem axles supplied to various chassis manufacturers. However they also have a division producing custom-built vehicles and this has been in business since 1915. Amongst its special products are fire-truck chassis marketed by International Harvester with International petrol (gasoline) or Detroit or Cummins diesel engines. Other vehicles include crane-carrying chassis, airfield trucks and tractors, oilfield trucks and refuse collection chassis.

Though most Hendricksons are for specialized off-road use the firm also makes highway models like this **H3** series 6 × 4 tractor. It can have various engines including 270, 325 and 360 bhp Caterpillar and equivalent Detroit diesels.

HINDUSTAN

Hindustan Motors Ltd
9/1 R. N. Mukherjee Road
Calcutta—700 001
India

Hindustan began by producing various American and British designs under licence, but since 1968 it has built virtually all its own components including engines for its larger trucks and buses based on Bedford designs. The normal-control J6 has standard Bedford styling but the forward-control variant is locally conceived. Smaller trucks are reminiscent of the Mini Moke but with rear-wheel drive.

J6 Forward Control has six-cylinder, 5408 cc (330 cu ins), 112 bhp diesel and four-speed gearbox. It is for 11,204 kg (24,700 lbs) GVW. Options include a five-speed gearbox and a petrol engine.

HINO

Hino Motors Ltd
7–17 Nihonbashi 1–chome
Chuo-ku
Tokyo 103
Japan

Hino's origins date from 1917 and they now make medium and heavy road vehicles as well as an extensive range of such specialized equipment as dumptrucks, fire appliances and mobile crane-carrying chassis. The firm has been owned by Toyota since 1967. Hino trucks are assembled by various overseas firms including J. Harris (Assemblers) Ltd in Cloghran, Ireland, who plan an English factory in 1980. Total annual Hino production is approximately 18,000.

ZM 704D 6×4 tipper chassis has tilt cab, ten-speed gearbox, and 14-litre, 295-bhp V-8 diesel. A normal-control version is also produced, as are maximum capacity forward-control artics with one or two driven axles.

IBEX

Ibex Manufacturing Inc
2331 So. 2300 W
Salt Lake City
Utah 84119
USA

Founded in 1964, Ibex specialized in tough off-highway
vehicles (named after the sure-footed ibex mountain
goat). It still custom builds such trucks today, though
a more recent development has been terminal tractors,
with elevating fifth wheels to suit a variety of trailers,
and also special trucks for loading aircraft. The latter
can be driven from either end, have mid-mounted engines, and bodies over their full length with the cabs
underneath.

F-2 terminal tractor has Ford, Detroit, Caterpillar or
Cummins engines of 145 to 215 bhp and Allison four-
or five-speed automatic transmissions. Its Rockwell
double reduction rear axle has a capacity of 29,000 lbs.

IFA

VEB IFA-Automobilwerke ·
172 Ludwigsfelde
German Democratic Republic

East German vehicle production under communist control was allocated to various new factories and ones that had previously made trucks, like Phänomen (see Robur). Heavy-vehicle production is now centred on Ludwigsfelde, where the IFA W50 is produced. The first W50 five-tonner was made in 1965, and, though a new design with MAN licence engine, it owed many features to the former Grube, which in turn was based on the Horch (a pre-communist partner in Auto Union). From 1979 Volvo were understood to be helping the modernization of the GDR truck industry.

IFA **W50** is available with 4×2 or 4×4 as a 5-tonne capacity rigid truck, fire appliance etc, or as an artic with IFA trailer. It has a four-cylinder, 6560 cc, 92 kW (125 bhp) diesel with MAN-licence combustion chamber. There is a five-speed gearbox with synchro on all but first. On this 4×4 model the axle drive shafts are located outside the load-carrying axle casings. The steel cab is fixed.

89

INTERNATIONAL

International Harvester Australia Ltd
211 Sturt Street
South Melbourne
Victoria 3205
Australia

International has long had a major share of the Australian truck market. On the strength of this it introduced
an Australian designed and built ACCO forward-control
range in 1964 and has since added a number of other
locally made models. Before Atkinson joined with Seddon in Britain it had a thriving Australian subsidiary also
making special trucks for local requirements. With the
takeover of Seddon Atkinson by International in 1974
the Australian Atkinson and International companies got
together and now their heavy vehicles are produced side
by side at a new plant at Danendong, Victoria. 1978
production totalled 5000 vehicles.

ACCO range covers 2-, 3- (including twin steer) and
4-axle models. Shown is an **F3074** 6 × 4 for 50 tonnes
(110,000 lbs) GTW with Roadranger fifteen-speed
gearbox and Cummins 903, 14.8-litre, 239 kW
(320 bhp) diesel. A steel tilt cab is fitted and a restyled
version is used on the new medium–heavy T-Line.

Though of American origin, this **SF 2670** has features to suit Australian requirements. It has a Cummins 261 kW diesel (350 bhp). The fibreglass bonnet hinges forward for access, and the chassis is of bolted construction. GCW is up to 54 tonnes.

Atkinsons have locally designed fibreglass cabs cushioned from the chassis by shock absorbers and quarter-elliptic springs. Detroit and Cummins diesels to 336 kW (450 bhp) are available with five- to twenty-speed gearboxes (some automatic, by Allison).

INTERNATIONAL

International Harvester Truck Division
401 North Michigan Avenue
Chicago
Illinois 60611
USA

As their name suggests International Harvester were originally farm machinery makers, but in 1907 their McCormick division started making IHC Auto-Buggies followed by Auto-Wagons in 1909. These were really motorized buckboards with enormous wheels and wide track to enable them to negotiate horsedrawn wagon trails. After 1914 all trucks were called International. They produce an indigenous ACCO range in Australia and own Seddon Atkinson in Britain and a part share in DAF and from 1980 in Pegaso as well (initially 35% rising to 65% in a new factory in 1983). Their designs are widely produced in South America.

S-Series includes four- and six-wheelers including 4×4 and 6×6. Depending on model, GVW covers 6713 kg (14,800 lbs) to 28,123 kg (62,000 lbs). Engines by International, Cummins, Detroit and Caterpillar are available from 112 kW (150 bhp) to 268 kW (360 bhp) with numerous transmission options.

Transstar Conventional is available as 4×2 or 6×4 for
GCW to 54,431 kg (120,000 lbs). Standard diesels are
Detroit 209 kW (280 bhp) or Cummins 216 kW
(290 bhp); ten- to sixteen-speed transmissions are
available.

Transtar CO is available as 4×2 or 6×4 with Cummins
engine as above standard and similar transmission
choice. There is widespread use of aluminium to save
weight. GCW is as above and GVW on 6×4 is up to
22,480 kg (49,560 lbs).

ISUZU

Isuzu Motors Ltd
22—10 Minamioi 6-chome
Shinagawaku
Tokyo
Japan 140

The forerunner of Isuzu made cars from 1916 and
Wolseley cars and trucks under licence from 1918 to
1927. The name Isuzu was adopted on its vehicles from
1934 and diesel vehicles made from 1941. Post-war production concentrated on trucks and cars, which, for
several years from 1953, were Hillman-based. Since
1971 Isuzu cars and commercials have been sold world-
wide by General Motors Corp (which owns 34% of
Isuzu) and Isuzu have assembled Chevrolet light commercials in Japan. Small pick-ups to large 6×6 trucks
are produced, total output of trucks in 1978 having been
18,000.

JCR for 12,500 kg (27,557 lbs) GVW is one of a range
of 2- and 3-axle trucks sharing the same steel tilt cab.
It has a five- or six-speed part synchro gearbox and two-
speed axle option. The six-cylinder, Isuzu, 5.785-litre
(353 cu ins) diesel develops 160 bhp gross.

SPZ for 26,000 kg (57,320 lbs) GVW has six-cylinder, 12-litre (733 cu ins) diesel developing 240 bhp gross and choice of transmissions including Fuller thirteen-speed. Other models sharing this steel tilt cab include 2-axle rigids and tractors and twin-steer six-wheelers.

TD range includes 2- and 3-axle models using either the 12-litre engine outlined above or, in smaller models, like this **TD50**, a six-cylinder, 10,179 cc (621 cu ins), 195 bhp diesel. GVW of this dumptruck is 16,000 kg (35,000 lbs). It has a five-speed, part synchro gearbox.

95

JELCZ

Jelczańskie Zakłady
  Samochodowe
Jelcz k/Oławy
Poland

The Jelcz factory has built trucks since 1960, though until 1968 these were called Zubr. Jelcz trucks use diesels built under licence from Leyland and Steyr, and Western technology is evident in other mechanical features as well as in the modern cab. Buses are built under licence from Berliet, and Jelcz builds special bodies on Star chassis, including mobile repair shops. Annual production of Jelcz trucks is reputed to be 6,000.

S 420 has GVW of 17,000 kg and GCW of 32,000 kg. It has a steel tilt cab and 11.1-litre 243 bhp, super-charged, six-cylinder diesel. A dual-range, six-speed, synchro gearbox is used.

96

KAELBLE

KAELBLE

Carl Kaelble GmbH
Postfach 1320
7150 Backnang
West Germany

Founded in 1884, Kaelble began to make road vehicles in 1926, having built up a reputation for railway locomotives (which it still produces). It has specialized in heavy road tractors and, since 1952, in dumptrucks. Recent developments have been crane-carriers, hot ingot and slag transporters, airfield crash tenders with engines up to 1100 bhp and earth-moving equipment and crawlers (including the recently acquired Gmeinder range).

Amongst an extensive range of heavy-haulage tractors is this 6×6 **KDVW 400S** for North Africa with Mercedes-Benz 294 kW (440 bhp) diesel and seven-man crew cab. It has planetary reduction in each wheel.

KENWORTH

Kenworth Truck Co
PO Box 80222
Seattle
Washington 98108
USA

Founded in 1915 as the Gerlinger Motor Company specializing in trucks for the logging industry, the name was changed to Kenworth in 1923 in honour of two stockholders, Kent and Worthington. The company has specialized in custom-built, heavy-duty vehicles ever since and in more recent years became part of the Paccar Group which also owns Peterbilt, Dart, Canadian Kenworth and from 1980, Foden.

Smaller than anything built by Kenworth in recent years is the new **W300** desert vehicle for 4536 kg (5-ton) payloads. It has 4×4, fibreglass bonnet and wings, Allison four-speed automatic gearbox with two-speed transfer box and Detroit 4-53T 126 kW (170 bhp) diesel.

Kenworth make a variety of giant 6×6 desert vehicles
of up to 700 bhp and 160,000 lbs GVW. Engines are by
Caterpillar, Cummins or Detroit and are cooled by over-
size vee-section radiators. The model shown has rollers
for loading over the tail by winch, mounted in the
behind-cab 'headache rack'.

Amongst a large range of forward- and normal-control
highway models is this 6×4 **K-100** available with steel
or aluminium chassis and proprietary leaf-spring rear
suspension or Kenworth's own air or torsion-bar sys-
tems. Tilt cab is of aluminium and fibreglass and there
are various weight-saving options like aluminium hubs,
fuel tanks etc and air in place of electric starter motor.
Most American proprietary engines can be specified.

KOCKUMS

Kockums Landsverk AB
Box 512
S-261 24 Landskrona
Sweden

Kockums' origins go back to 1864 and it became an important supplier of railway carriages. From 1925 it produced military vehicles and later tanks. After World War II it developed crawler excavators and in 1957 development of a range of dumptrucks began. In 1979 the Swedish State Company took over the transport division and it is now integrated with another subsidiary, Kalmar, which makes fork-lift trucks amongst other things and has produced commercial vehicles in the past. Another branch of Kockums makes forestry vehicles, on which 4 × 4 and 6 × 6 pivot-steer dumptrucks are based. In addition Kockum Landsverk makes 25- to 45-ton rigid dumptrucks with Scania, Cummins and Detroit diesel engines.

442B can carry 32,000 kg (35 tons) and has a Scania V-8, 295 kW, 401 gross bhp, diesel and Allison five-speed, automatic transmission. Final drive is by planetary gearing in the rear wheels. Only the front axle has suspension (by leaf springs) though most other models have all-wheel, oleo-pneumatic suspension.

KOMATSU

Komatsu Ltd
No. 3–6 2-chome Akasaka
Minato-ku
Tokyo
Japan

Komatsu started making mining machinery in 1921 and by 1932 were producing crawler tractors. These led to interest in construction machinery, including excavators, bulldozers and dumptrucks, and recently licensing arrangements have been made to build American machines in Japan. Following an agreement with Cummins Engines of America in 1961 most are powered by locally built versions of their diesels. Other forms of commercial vehicles made by Komatsu are three varieties of tracked snow vehicles which have been used in Antarctica, heavy-duty aircraft and dock tractors and 3-axle slag-carrying trucks. Komatsu built their first dumptruck in 1951. It was of 15 tonnes capacity whereas today's range covers machines of 20 to 132 tons (US) capacity.

HD680–2 is for payloads of 68 tonnes (75 US tons) and has Cummins V-12, 28-litre (1710 cu ins), 775 bhp diesel. It has torque converter transmission with six-speed planetary gearbox, disc brakes on the rear axle (drum brakes at front) and hydro-pneumatic suspension front and rear (independent suspension at front).

LEADER

Leader Trucks Australia Pty Ltd
c/o HW Crouch Pty Ltd
Sydney
NSW
Australia

A new name in Australian trucking using American-origin proprietary components is the Leader, whose makers have been involved in road transport for forty years. Four-, six- and eight-wheel Leaders are produced utilizing Caterpillar diesels. Fuller or Allison gearboxes, and Hendrickson suspended Rockwell tandems. Although resembling the steel-cabbed Hino, the Leader in fact has a fibreglass cab.

A8 208 Mid Ranger has a 10.4-litre (636 cu in) Caterpillar V-8 diesel, developing 149 kW (200 bhp), and thirteen-speed manual or four- or five-speed automatic transmission. GCW is 27,275 kg.

LECTRA HAUL

Unit Rig and Equipment Co
PO Box 3107
Tulsa
Oklahoma 74101
USA

Unit Rig has made over 1200 giant diesel-electric dump-trucks since it first introduced the Lectra Haul in 1963. It also makes aircraft tow tractors and 60-ton capacity fork-lift trucks. The dumptrucks are 2-axle machines of 85–200-ton capacity and an articulated 180-ton bottom dump is also produced. Caterpillar, Cummins, Detroit and EMD diesels of up to 2475 bhp drive dynamos which in turn power rear-wheel motors. The wheel motors also provide dynamic braking. A recent development has been 145-tonne bottom dumps with four abreast wheels at front and rear.

Mark 36 can carry 154 tonnes (170 short tons) and has 1600 bhp diesel driving an alternator which provides current to rear-wheel motors. It has resilient block suspension and a heaped body capacity of up to 121 cu m (158 cu yds). The wheel motors can be switched to generators to provide dynamic retarding and there are, in addition, disc brakes at front and rear.

LEYLAND

Leyland Vehicles Ltd
Lancaster House
Leyland
Preston PR5 1SN
Lancashire
England

Commercial vehicles have been made at Leyland since 1897 and the company is now one of the world's largest producers. Leyland acquired Albion in 1951, Scammell in 1955, AEC in 1962, Bristol trucks in 1965, Rover/Alvis in 1966 and Aveling-Barford in 1967. Then in 1968 came the merger with British Motor Holdings, parent company of Austin, Morris, Guy and Daimler (to name only the commercials). This near-nationalized firm has replaced many of the older names with Leyland. A small selection is shown, while the immense variety includes many others over one ton. Other Leylands are produced in Turkey, Iran, India, Kenya, Australia etc.

Boxer range covers rigids for 9.84 to 16 tons plus a 20-tonne GCW artic. They have five-speed (synchro on top four ratios) gearboxes (auto optional on some) and Leyland six-cylinder, 5.65-litre diesel developing 109 bhp (137 when turbocharged). The cab tilts and a two-speed axle is optional.

Bison 2 is one of several models using the Ergomatic tilt cab. It has 6×4 and is for a GVW of 24,390 kg (24 tons). It is particularly popular in the construction industry and can have Leyland 11.1- or 12.47-litre, six-cylinder diesels developing 181 to 209 bhp. Six- or nine-speed gearboxes are used.

Marathon 2 is most familiar as an artic. The range has Leyland, Cummins or Rolls-Royce diesels of up to 290 bhp and various transmission options. GCW is up to 38 tonnes (65 tonnes GTW) or 32 tons GCW in the UK.

Landtrain was new in 1980 and primarily for export. It is available with 4×2 or 6×4 and Leyland or Cummins diesels of 212 to 290 bhp with six- or nine-speed gearboxes. GVW of 4×2 is 19 tonnes and of 6×4 30 tonnes. GTW of each is up to 40 and 65 tonnes respectively.

Roadtrain was also new in 1980 using a Motor Panels tilt cab that will spread to a whole range of 6.5- to 65-tonne models and retain 60% parts commonality. **16.28** model shown is for 32 tons GCW in UK and has new Leyland six-cylinder, TL12 Flexitorque 12.47-litre diesel developing 270 bhp net and ten-speed, constant-mesh, Spicer splitter gearbox. Proprietary engines are also available.

LIAZ

Liberecké Automobilové Závody (LIAZ)
46605 Jablonec nad Nisou
Czechoslovakia

Škoda's roots go back to 1906, when Laurin & Klement began to build vehicles in Prague. In 1924 they became an integral part of the new Škoda company. Škoda's heavy vehicles, as opposed to car-derived light vans, have been made at the LIAZ factory since about 1950 and this name now appears on many of their vehicles. Karosa buses and coaches use Škoda/LIAZ components and are made at Bysoké Myto. All these vehicles, as well as the products of Tatra, are exported by Motokov, Prague.

The LIAZ **100.05** is part of a range of international vehicles which include the similar 100.45 articulated tractor. They have 200 kW (270 bhp) or 222 kW (304 bhp) turbocharged (Holset turbocharger) six-cylinder diesels and two-range, five-speed gearboxes. GTW of up to 38,000 kg is permissible.

MACK

Mack Trucks Inc.
PO Box M, Allentown
Pennsylvania 18105
USA

Mack was a wagon-building firm which produced trucks and buses from 1900. The company expanded after merging with the American licensees of the Swiss Saurer in 1911, and in 1915 introduced the famous Bulldog range of trucks, well known for their radiators mounted behind sloping bonnets, which stayed in production until 1939. They now make a wide range of heavy-duty trucks as well as fire-engines and dump-trucks. They use Caterpillar, Cummins, Detroit and their own high-torque Maxidyne engines, which, because of near constant horsepower developed through a wide rev band, can have fewer gearbox ratios. The smaller models use Mack diesels based on Scania designs.

In 1979 Mack acquired the plant that assembled their trucks in Australia and in the same year Renault bought a 20% stake in the American firm and are to supply medium-weight diesel trucks to be sold as Macks in the USA with locally fitted transmissions.

WL/WS Series Cruise-Liner built in California for West Coast operation has aluminium cab and large radiator to suit most sizes of Maxidyne or proprietary engine. For similar high-power haulage with normal-control, Mack make the RW Series Super Liner.

108

DM Series is available for GVW up to 46,700 kg (103,000 lbs) with diesels of up to 336 kW (450 bhp). Primarily for the construction industry, it can have the steel bonnet shown here or, for less arduous service, a forward-tilting fibreglass front. An oil bath long-life clutch is available for short-haul work.

The manoeuvrable, short-haul, 2-axle, city tractor and fire appliance chassis (MC model) and front-loading six-wheel refuse chassis (**MR** model, shown here) share this new steel tilt cab. Mack, Caterpillar and Mack-Scania diesels of 149 to 213 kW (200 to 285 bhp) are available and the ladder gives access to the hydraulic loading mechanism.

MAGIRUS DEUTZ

Klöckner-Humboldt-Deutz AG
Werk Ulm, 7900 Ulm/Donau
West Germany

Magirus started by making horse-drawn fire-engines in 1864 and produced its first goods vehicles in 1916. In 1935 it joined forces with the Humboldt machinery firm and the Deutz engine-making company (whose co-founder Otto had invented the four-stroke cycle in 1876). From 1940 KHD developed air-cooled engines, which became their hallmark in post-war vehicles. Today Magirus Deutz produce buses, fire engines, on- and off-road transport vehicles and municipal chassis. With Fiat and its subsidiaries, Lancia, OM and Unic they are members of the joint IVECO (Industrial Vehicles Corporation BV) and there is considerable interchange of components and ideas between them. Magirus Deutz are also involved at a technical level with the Club of Four (DAF, Saviem, Volvo and themselves) in the development of middleweight models.

256.19 FL has air-cooled, V-8, 12,763 cc, 188 kW (256 bhp) diesel and is for 19 tonnes GVW. It has eight-speed ZF or thirteen-speed Roadranger gearbox and the example shown has tilt sleeper cab and air suspension on its rear axle.

A new version of the familiar normal-control Magirus Deutz site vehicle is this **192 M16**, 16-tonne GVW, 4×4 tipper with 9572 cc, V-6, 141 kW (192 bhp), air-cooled diesel.

New in 1979, but not entering series production until 1981, is the low-profile **DL 30 nB** turntable escape. It has an overall height of 2.85 m and its 141 or 188 kW (192 or 256 bhp) diesel is mounted behind its cab. The entire vehicle including ladder is made by Magirus.

310 D 32 AK working at 50 degrees centigrade in the Tunisian desert. GTW is 60 tonnes. Latest 320 version has V-10, 235 kW (320 bhp) diesel. As a rigid the 6× 6 truck has a GVW of 32 tonnes.

Magirus Deutz **light range** covers 5.13 to 7.9 tonnes and all share the same model of four-cylinder, 64 kW (87 bhp), air-cooled, Deutz diesel with five-speed, synchro gearbox. They are available as chassis/cab (or crew cab) or 10.6 to 16.8 cu m vans.

MAN

Maschinenfabrik Augsburg-Nürnberg AG
Postfach 500620
8000 München 50
West Germany

MAN, an engineering firm dating from the 19th century, built its first diesel truck in 1924. It has continued to concentrate on diesel-engined trucks and buses and in 1971 took over Büssing Automobilwerke. MAN has a reciprocal sales arrangement with Saviem-Renault for marketing each other's medium (Saviem) and heavy (MAN) ranges, and have close links with ÖAF and Gräf & Stift. Their vehicles and engines are also made under licence in various countries. They have some technical links with Mercedes-Benz and are joint owners with them of the MTU large diesel and turbine firm. In 1979 MAN–VW introduced a joint mid range.

MAN–VW covers 6–9 tonnes GVW (14.5-tonner from 1981) and has MAN 3.8-litre, four-cylinder or 5.7-litre, six-cylinder diesels and VW five-speed gearbox and cab derived from LT models. The smallest **6.90 FK** is shown with four-cylinders, 66 kW (90 bhp) diesel.

MAN produce 2- and 3-axle, semi-forward-control models and this **30.240 DHS** example has a six-cylinder, 177 kW (240 bhp) diesel. Its GVW is 30 tonnes and GTW over 40 tonnes. Turbocharged 206 and 235 kW (280 and 320 bhp) are also available.

Forward-control MAN range covers numerous models up to 150 tonnes GTW with engines of up to 294 kW (400 bhp). Shown is a **19.280** rigid with drawbar trailer operating at 38 tonnes GCW. It has a six-cylinder, 206 kW (280 bhp), turbocharged diesel. Roadranger and ZF gearboxes with up to sixteen forward ratios are available.

MARMON

Marmon Motor Co
PO Box 5175
Dallas
Texas 75222
USA

The Marmon name first appeared on a famous line of American cars which culminated in a V-16 luxury model in 1931. It then appeared on Marmon-Herrington off-road trucks and all-wheel drive conversions to existing vehicles. In 1963 the Marmon name and manufacturing rights to a new on-highway truck were sold to the new Marmon Motor Co. Meanwhile the old Marmon-Herrington firm, trading as Marmon Transmotive, continues to make small quantities of off-highway and utility trucks in Knoxville, Tennessee, as well as all-wheel drive conversion kits for mass-produced trucks. The Marmon Motor Co has increased its own production to approximately 1000 lightweight heavy-duty tractors per year which mostly go to owner-drivers.

Cabover and conventional models with aluminium cabs and other lightweight components are produced with Caterpillar, Cummins or Detroit diesels, mostly in the 335 to 430 bhp range. Most extras like CB radio and stereo tape player are included in the basic specification.

MAXIM

Maxim Motor Division
Middleboro
Massachusetts 02346
USA

Maxim has made fire equipment since 1888 and began to produce self-propelled fire-engines during World War I. They were amongst the first American fire-engine makers to provide shaft drive and pneumatic tyres. Today they make cabover and conventional (forward- and normal-control) chassis including articulated aerial ladder models. The firm was for a time a division of Seagrave (now part of FWD) but, during the seventies, Maxim separated and now leaves its international marketing to Ward LaFrance. Various engines from 236 to 435 bhp are available with 1000 to 2000 gpm pumps.

Maxim Marauder with 236 bhp diesel and 33,280 lbs GVW. Top speed is 60 mph and it has 1000 gpm two-stage pump with 500-gallon booster tank and steel and aluminium body and cab which can incorporate numerous custom options.

MAZDA

Toyo Kogyo Co Ltd
6047 Fuchu-Machi
Aki-gun
Hiroshima
Japan

Toyo Kogyo began to produce light, motor-cycle based commercial vehicles in 1931. Small vans and pick-ups, based on car components, are produced today, although the Mazda range has recently extended into slightly larger diesel trucks of around 2 tons capacity. Ford has links with Mazda and their Ford Trader 3-tonner for the Australian market is made by Mazda.

The largest tilt-cab, forward-control Mazda models can have 2000 cc petrol or 2700 or 3700 cc diesel engines developing 81.92 and 100 bhp respectively. In each case payload is around 2000 kg and an unusual feature is box-section chassis rails. The largest-engined **Titan** model is shown.

MEILI

Meili Fahrzeugbau AG
March-Werk
8862 Schübelbach SZ
Switzerland

Starting out by manufacturing farm tractors in 1932, Meili switched to the small truck business in 1964. Today two basic models are produced with 3.5-ton and 7-ton GVW and 4×4 drive. The narrow construction is designed especially for mountain roads and small urban streets. A large variety of bodies and options are available such as: snow ploughs, street sweepers, street-washers, tankers, tippers, garbage collectors. Meili also sell the larger Sirmac cross-country vehicle in Switzerland and are Hino concessionaires.

MA 4000, 80 bhp, 4-cylinder Perkins diesel, carrying lubrication tank and equipment for 7-ton GVW, 4×4 drive with five-speed plus reverse gearbox with one- or two-range transfer box giving up to fifteen forward gears.

MERCEDES-BENZ

Daimler-Benz AG
Stuttgart-Untertürkheim
West Germany

Daimler and Benz merged in 1926, having made their first commercial vehicles in 1895 and 1896 respectively. Benz was one of the diesel-engine pioneers, running a diesel truck as early as 1923, whilst Daimler made the world's first practical four-wheel car in 1886. Mercedes-Benz is Germany's largest producer of commercial vehicles, having absorbed Hanomag—Henschel in the early seventies. It has technical links with MAN and Steyr (with whom it also has commercial links) and produces light vans to heavy-haulage vehicles, off-road Unimog vehicles and various buses and coaches. It also produces commercial vehicles in Brazil, Argentina, South Africa, Spain, Turkey, Iran and Indonesia. Mercedes-Benz trucks are also assembled in the USA (6000 per year in Hampton, Virginia), and their Unimog range is also marketed in the USA by Case, the farm tractor makers. In 1977 Mercedes acquired White's Euclid division.

LP 1113 from the Wörth factory can carry 7170 kg. Its model code indicates 11 tonnes GVW and 130 bhp (96 kW). It is the largest of the LP range which start at 5.9 tonnes GVW and 63 kW (85 bhp).

Unimog 1300 L 4×4 vehicle equipped for tackling forest fires. It has a turbocharged, 96 kW (130 bhp), six-cylinder diesel and comes from a wide variety of Unimogs ranging in power from 38 to 124 kW (52 to 168 bhp).

Two varieties of panel van from a range suitable for 2- to 6.5-tonne loads and a volume of up to 20 cu m. Power steering and automatic transmission are available. On the left is a **613 D** example from the Düsseldorf range and on the right a **307 D** Bremen van, both named after the factory in which they were produced. Bremen is the one-time home of Borgward, part of whose plant was bought by Hanomag.

1628 can be a rigid (when its GVW is 16 tonnes) or tractor and has a new 206 kW (280 bhp), V-8, 14.62-litre diesel and ZF eight-speed or Roadranger thirteen-speed gearbox. The engine is designed to give high torque rise to boost pulling power as engine speed drops.

1638 is for 16 tonnes GVW and 38 tonnes GTW. The engine is a turbocharged version of the V-8 in the 1628 and develops 276 kW (375 bhp). A 6×4 2238 version is also available.

MITSUBISHI

Mitsubishi Motors Corporation
33—8, 5-chome Shiba
Minato-ku
Tokyo
Japan

Mitsubishi, which means 'Three Diamonds' in Japanese, started over 100 years ago in the shipping and heavy engineering industries. They assembled their first car in 1917 followed by a bus in 1932. In 1935 they made Japan's first diesel commercials. The motor vehicle division became an independent company in 1970 and the following year Chrysler bought a 15% share, which amongst other advantages enables them to sell Colt light vehicles in America as Dodge Colts. Mitsubishi's heavy vehicles are named Fuso and they also produce Caterpillar equipment under licence in Japan. In 1978 Mitsubishi produced approximately 15,000 Fuso commercial vehicles, ranging in size from medium trucks to 430 bhp, heavy-haulage tractors and dumptrucks. In 1980 their links with US Dodge were reported to be ending.

Fuso crane-carrier has 4×2 and a 215 bhp diesel. It is for cranes of around 15 tons capacity. Mitsubishi's smaller diesel engines are supplied for use by Chrysler in the US. Chrysler also import the Dodge D-50/Plymouth Arrow pick-ups from Mitsubishi.

MOL

MOL NV
Diksmuidesteenweg 63
B 8830 Hooglede
Belgium

Well known for bodywork and trailers since World War
II, Mol added all-wheel drive, Deutz-engined, normal-
control tippers to its products in the mid sixties and has
proceeded to develop a very wide range of special-purpose vehicles since then. It now produces 'dock spotter'
ro-ro tractors, crane-carriers and heavy-haulage and off-
road trucks, as well as Eagle coaches (a firm that it
acquired in the late seventies). Most of its vehicles have
Deutz air-cooled engines.

38-tonne GVW Mol refrigerated artic outfit with
DAF six-cylinder turbocharged, 11,600 cc, 191 kW
(260 bhp) diesel and ZF six-speed gearbox. A similar
three-point rubber suspended cab is used on much of
Mol's normal-control 4×2, 6×4 and 6×6 range.

123

Mol make chassis for truck-mounted cranes of from 75 to 300 tonnes capacity with 3, 4, 5 or 6 axles. This **12 × 6** example has a Deutz V-10, 300 bhp diesel and ZF six-speed gearbox. Top speed is 60 km/h.

T6066 'Giant' has Deutz V-12, 17-litre, 390 bhp diesel and torque converter transmission with eight forward and four reverse ratios. GCW is up to 258,500 kg (570,000 lbs) on the road and 129,500 kg (285,000 lbs) on desert sand, where many are used for moving oilfield equipment.

124

NISSAN

Nissan Motor Co Ltd
17–1 Ginza 6-chome
Chuo-Ku
Tokyo
Japan

Nissan Diesel Motor Co Ltd
3–7–1 Kanda Nishiki-cho
Chiyoda-ku
Tokyo
Japan

Nissan has existed since 1934 and controls Datsun, whose cars and light commercials are outside the scope of this book. Since 1955 it has had close ties with heavy truck maker Minsei Diesel, which in 1980 was 48% owned by Nissan and known as the Nissan Diesel Motor Co. It produces all Nissan's heavy models and special-purpose trucks and uses its own engines of up to 18 litres (V-10) capacity. Nissan has owned Prince Motors since 1966 and continues to make certain of its medium-weight models, notably the Homer, amongst its own light and medium models. In 1980 Nissan bought a 36% interest in the makers of Ebro vehicles in Spain.

Nissan **Clipper** for loads of 2000 kg (4410 lbs) started life in Prince range. It can have 1982 cc petrol or 2164 cc, four-cylinder diesel engines developing 91 and 66 gross bhp respectively. It has four- or five-speed synchromesh transmission.

Nissan Diesel **TFA21** is 4×4 truck with six-cylinder, 185 bhp diesel 15,400 kg (33,950 lbs) GVW. A five-speed, constant-mesh or synchro gearbox is available with two-speed transfer box. Nissan diesel also makes 2-axle dumptrucks to 350 bhp for 23-ton loads.

Nissan Diesel **CD10** is a 6×2 haulage model with tilt cab. GVW is 21 tonnes (46,300 lbs) and 6842 cc, six-cylinder diesel develops 160 bhp. It has a five-speed, part synchro gearbox.

126

ÖAF

Österreichische Automobilfabrik
ÖAF-Gräf & Stift AG
Postfach 93
1211 Vienna
Austria

The company started in 1907 as Austro-Fiat to produce
Italian designs under licence. It gradually developed its
own vehicles from 1921 and after World War II changed
its name from AF to ÖAF. It is now merged with Gräf
& Stift and has close ties with the German MAN company. Many of its vehicles are licence-built MAN's, but
under a reciprocal arrangement its own ÖAF Jumbo
vehicles are sold in various countries as MAN Jumbos.

Jumbo 40 400 is for 40 tonnes GVW and up to 250
tonnes GCW. It has a MAN tilt cab with or without
sleeping compartment and a MAN V-10, 15,953 cc,
294 kW (400 bhp) diesel. It has 6×6 and six-speed, Allison automatic or eight-speed ZF manual gearbox plus
transfer box.

OM

OM
Fiat SpA
10 Corso Marconi
Turin 10100
Italy

The first truck bearing the initials OM was made in 1918, though one of the group of companies which combined to create SA Officine Meccaniche (literally Work Shop Ltd) had earlier made railway equipment and a few lorries. Early OM trucks were based on Saurer designs and as a result OM was involved at an early stage with diesel engines. In 1938 they were acquired by Fiat, who gradually rationalized their models, so that today, as joint members of IVECO, their trucks are identical except in badge, sometimes model name, and in marketing and servicing network. OM's speciality within IVECO is to make a group of 90 to 130 bhp, water-cooled diesels, as well as gearboxes, axles and forward-control cabs.

150.14 is for 15 tonnes GVW and has a six-cylinder, 103 kW (140 bhp) diesel and five-speed gearbox. Single or double reduction or two-speed rear axles are available. The cab tilts and is a derivative from the heavy vehicle range of IVECO.

128

OSHKOSH

Oshkosh Truck Corp
PO Box 2566
2307 Oregon St
Oshkosh
Wisconsin 54903
USA

Founded in 1917 to make all-wheel drive trucks for use on America's rural tracks and in difficult winter conditions. Oshkosh trucks soon earned a reputation for go-anywhere capabilities that made them popular in timber, snow ploughing, oil-drilling, fire-fighting and heavy-haulage operations. Today Oshkosh also produce standard highway trucks using Caterpillar engines.

P, R, F and J Series share similar cabs and are heavy-duty 6×4 and 6×6 models, sometimes with tag axles to reduce ground pressure. Shown is an **R 6 × 4** available with 210 to 270 kW (280 to 360 bhp) diesels and nine- to thirteen-speed gearboxes with option of two-speed auxiliary box. It is transporting a giant **J 6 × 6** desert model available with engines of up to 336 kW (450 bhp) and wide choice of manual and automatic gearboxes. Rear tandem capacity is up to 31,752 kg (70,000 lbs) and front axle 12,247 kg (27,000 lbs).

129

Oshkosh makes 4×4 and 8×8 airport crash tenders. This
is the **M-23** equipped with front- and rear-mounted
Detroit V-8 diesels totalling 734 kW (984 bhp) and twin
five-speed automatic gearboxes with torque converters.
It carries 22,712 litres (6000 galls) water plus 1949 litres
(515 galls) of foam and can discharge at the rate of
6813 lpm (1800 gpm). It can reach its top speed of
80 km/h (50 mph) in 55 seconds.

B Series front-discharge concrete transit mixer has 6×4
or 6×6 with additional self-steering hydraulically raisable tag axle. Choice of 157 to 217 kW (210 to 290 bhp)
diesels are mounted at the rear and four-/five-speed
automatic or six-/ten-speed manual gearboxes are
available.

130

OTTAWA

Daybrook Ottawa Corp
1313 North Hickory Street
Ottawa
Kansas
USA

Ottawa is probably the USA's best-known maker of 'yard spotters', terminal tractors, ro-ro tractors and similar vehicles designed to take the place of long-distance artic units in dockyards and truck depots. Several models also comply with highway regulations and are used for short-haul, semi-trailer movement on the road.

Ottawa **C-50** half-cab tractive unit for 50 tons GTW. Various proprietary transmission and engine options are available, as is an elevating fifth wheel to suit various trailer heights.

PACIFIC

Pacific Truck and Trailer Ltd
PO Box 2084
Vancouver
British Columbia V6B 3T2
Canada

Pacific started by making logging trucks and trailers in 1947 and was acquired by International Harvester Co of Canada Ltd in 1970. International now offer world-wide sales and parts but leave Pacific design and manufacture to the 200 employees in North Vancouver. Pacific makes very heavy-duty 6×6 and 6×4 tractors and trucks for the logging, sugar cane, construction, ore extraction and indivisible load haulage industries. They have Detroit, Cummins or Caterpillar diesel engines.

Pacific recently introduced a conventional **'Canadian'** highway range with International cab but their own steel or fibreglass (shown here) bonnet. Various Cummins, Detroit and Caterpillar engines are available up to 450 bhp with numerous transmission options. Rear tandems up to 80,000 lbs capacity can be specified.

132

P-16 6×4 logging tractor has Detroit 852 cu ins, 475 bhp, V-12 diesel (other Detroit, Cummins and Caterpillar engines of up to 700 bhp available), Allison automatic transmission and water-cooled brakes (400-gallon tank capacity). The Clark rear tandem axles have a capacity of 100,000 lbs.

Pacific make various sizes of Roughneck oilfield vehicles with 6×6. This **P-12-W** has 475 bhp Detroit diesel and eight-speed gearbox with torque converter. Its unladen weight is 23,179 kg (51,100 lbs).

PEGASO

Comercial Pegaso SA
General Sanjurjo 2
Madrid 4
Spain

The first Pegaso was made by Empresa Nacional de Autocamiones SA (Enasa) in 1946 in the former factory of the famous Hispano-Suiza car firm. They used many Leyland components and in 1966 their controlling company, Enasa, took over Sava, who had produced Austin commercial vehicles under licence in Spain. They now have a production capacity of around seventy vehicles per day comprising both buses, coaches and four-, six- and eight-wheel trucks. 850 kg to 6-ton models are by Sava whilst Pegaso covers the 6- to 38-ton range. In 1980 International Harvester acquired a 35% stake in Pegaso and intend to have a majority share in a new factory opening in 1983.

1101 retains traditional Pegaso fixed cab and is for 10.7 tonnes GVW. It has a 4370 cc, four-cylinder, 66 kw (90 bhp) diesel and six-speed gearbox. It is used primarily for municipal duties.

1121 with the tilt cab (available with sleeping compartment) which is used on Pegaso's medium and heavy range. The 1121 has a six-cylinder, 6550 cc, 99 kW (135 bhp) diesel and six-speed gearbox and is for 14.2 tonnes GVW.

3076D and **3078** dumptrucks have 6×4 and 6×6 respectively and are for up to 36,000 kg GVW. They have turbocharged, 10,518 cc, six-cylinder, diesels developing 191 kW (260 bhp) and two-range, four-speed or nine-speed gearboxes.

PERLINI

Perlini International
Viale dell' Industria
37047 San Bonifacio
Verona
Italy

Perlini made its first dumptruck in 1962, its thousandth in 1970 and its five thousandth in 1978. In 1971 airfield crash-tender chassis were added to the range and today Perlini employs over 1400 making these and dumptrucks of 22 to 85 short tons capacity.

DP 205 has Detroit V-6, 9050 cc, 206 kW (238 bhp) diesel and ZF six-speed gearbox. Both axles have oleo-pneumatic suspension and payload is 22,000 kg.

DP 855 has Detroit V-16, 24,141 cc, 800 bhp diesel (720 bhp optional) and Allison six-speed powershift transmission. There is oleo-pneumatic suspension on both axles and payload is 77,000 kg (170,000 lbs).

605 D 4×4 crash-tender chassis with fire equipment by Baribbi. It has twin rear-mounted, Detroit V-6 diesels totalling 530 bhp and five-speed, Allison automatic transmission. Top speed is 100 km/h and 80 km/h can be reached in 45 seconds.

PETERBILT

Peterbilt Motors Company
38801 Cherry Street
Newark
California
USA

Peterbilt grew from the remnants of the Fageol company
in Oakland, California, in 1939 and produces custom-
built on- and off-highway, forward- and normal-control
machines. These include 'California Haulers' able to
withstand the long inclines and rugged climate of the
West Coast states. Peterbilt is now associated with Kenworth in the Paccar group, which they joined in 1958.

Model **310** is the smallest Peterbilt with low-mounted
aluminium cab to suit short-haul work including front-
load refuse collection, Various Cummins and Caterpillar
engines are available and there is an automatic transmission option.

138

Model **352** is available as 4×2 or 6×4 with Cummins 14,005 cc (855 cu ins), 350 gross bhp diesel and thirteen-speed with overdrive Fuller Roadranger gearbox. An H version is available with Caterpillar 450 gross bhp diesel and all share the same aluminium tilt cab with other aluminium component options.

Model **353** covers various 6×4 and 6×6 rigids and tractors for tough operating conditions. They have steel and aluminium cab, Cummins 350 gross bhp diesel, fifteen-speed Fuller gearbox and 24,970 kg (55,000 lbs) rear suspension capacity.

139

PEUGEOT

PSA Peugeot–Citroën
75 Avenue de la Grande Armée
75116 Paris
France

Peugeot has made commercial vehicles based on its car engines and other components since the 1890s, and up to the 1920s also made a heavy vehicle range. Peugeot's 1950s forward-control van was a Chenard-Walcker design that they acquired along with that company. A more recent acquisition was of Citroën-Berliet in late 1974 (though Berliet was subsequently hived off to Renault) and then, in 1978, they purchased Chrysler's European car and truck manufacturing facilities and so control the Dodge plants in France (ex Simca), Spain and Britain. Citroën-Peugeot is also collaborating with Fiat on a van factory in southern Italy.

The Peugeot **J7** with front-wheel drive, which allows a wide choice of wheelbase lengths without many mechanical changes, and even conversion to 3-axle low-loaders. The standard model has all-round independent suspension, choice of petrol or diesel engines of approximately 1600 to 2200 cc and payloads to 1800 kg.

PIRSCH

Peter Pirsch & Sons Co
1308-35th Street
Kenosha
Wisconsin 53141
USA

Having developed a special fire-fighting ladder in 1899
Pirsch began to equip truck chassis with fire equipment.
In 1926 they built their first complete vehicle and today
build on both their own custom chassis and on proprietary makes. Their first forward-control model came
in 1961, since when most vehicles have been of this
configuration.

Custom **88D** rear-mounted aerial ladder truck with
100 ft Pirsch four-section ladder. Various engine/trans-
mission options are available. Note the Onan diesel
auxiliary generator.

PRP

Groupe Empain
Division Creusot-Loire
Paris
France

This firm's truck-making origins go back to 1919 when Willème started to recondition American Liberty trucks. From these it developed its own models which continued to bear the Willème name until the late seventies. In latter years they have been extra-heavy-duty types. In 1971 the company name was acquired by Perez et Raimond, Paris (PRP), which had also started in business by reconditioning US military vehicles (though this time World War II types) and had gone on to make such specialized vehicles as crane-carriers. In 1979 PRP was acquired by the industrial group Creusot-Loire, whose other truck involvement is making VAB 4×4 and 6×6 armoured military vehicles in association with Renault.

T 40 A 8×6, 40-tonne capacity tank transporter has demountable body and choice of Detroit, Cummins, Caterpillar or Mercedes-Benz diesels in the 300 to 450 bhp range with Allison automatic or Fuller thirteen-speed manual transmissions. The vehicle is also available as a 200-tonne tractive unit.

PUMA

Puma Industria de Veiculos SA
Av Presidente Wilson 4385
CP 42.649
São Paulo
Brazil

Puma began by producing sports cars in 1968 based
on locally produced VW running gear. This car and a
fibreglass-bodied sports saloon were soon joined by 4-
tonne capacity trucks with Perkins or MWM engines and
steel-framed, fibreglass cabs. Other components are of
largely US origin.

Puma **4T** has 83 bhp, four-cylinder diesels by MWM
(3922 cc) or Perkins (3860 cc) and four-speed Clark
transmission. The rear axle is by Brazilian Rockwell. It
has a steel-framed, fibreglass cab and GVW is 6000 kg.

143

RÁBA

Magyar Vagon-és Gépgyár
H-9002 Györ Pf 50
Hungary

The Wagon and Machinery Works at Györ was in Austria until after World War I and made commercial vehicles from as early as 1910. Since World War II it has concentrated on licence-built foreign vehicles, originally from Krupp and ÖAF. but since 1970 from the latter company's German partner, MAN. 4×2, 6×2, 6×4 and 6×6 vehicles are made all with MAN-licence diesels and Rába axles.

26.230 three-way tippers can have 6×6 or 6×4. They have six- or twelve-speed gearboxes. 230 bhp, 10,694 cc, six-cylinder MAN-licence diesels and have a GVW of 26 tonnes. The steel cab tilts.

RAM

R. A. Mimiasie NV
Hoofdweg 123
Rotterdam
Netherlands

Like Terberg and Ginaf, RAM began by modernizing American ex-army vehicles for use as off-road tippers, etc. Now that these old components are more or less used up, RAM purchases new components from various sources.

6 × 6 tipper uses Saviem/Renault tilt cab, Belgian-built MAN 797 diesel, MAN and Rockwell axles and a synchromesh, ZF, five-speed gearbox.

145

RAMIREZ

Trailers de Monterrey SA
Ave Universidad al Norte
Apdo Postal 437
Monterrey NL
Mexico

Trailers de Monterrey have made trailers for many years and some ten years ago decided that they could equally well produce haulage units from well-known proprietary American components. The resulting Ramirez R20 has a locally produced fibreglass cab and tilt bonnet. The seats fold flat pneumatically for sleeping. Ramirez also produce a small 4×4 utility vehicle with GMC 136 bhp petrol engine.

Ramirez **R20** tractor can carry an imposed load of 10,000 kg on its fifth wheel coupling. It has a Mexican-built Cummins six-cylinder, 230 bhp diesel. Eaton rear axle and Fuller gearbox.

RELIANCE-MERCURY

Reliance-Mercury Ltd
Mile Cross Works
Gibbet Street
Halifax
West Yorkshire HX1 4JQ
England

Reliance and Mercury were both specialists in industrial, port and airfield trucks and tractors who merged in 1972. Prior to that Mercury, which was founded in 1920, had been a subsidiary of Dennis for some eight years. Now members of the Marshalls Halifax Group, the combined firm makes a wide range of tractors outside the scope of this book and the Haulmajor ro-ro tractor for handling semi-trailers at ports and goods depots.

Haulmajor has elevating fifth wheel of 25 tons capacity and Leyland 155 or 180 bhp, turbocharged diesels. Drive to the Kirkstall hub reduction rear axle is via a Clark Powershift three forward and three reverse speed gearbox. The cab can be mounted to left or right and have duplicated controls for travelling forwards and backwards if required. GTW is 70 tons.

RENAULT

Renault Véhicules Industriels
33 Quai Galliéni
BP 100
92153 Suresnes Cedex
France

Renault's heavy vehicles were produced under the Saviem name between 1955 and 1979, but in an effort to integrate these with the Berliet range (Berliet was acquired by Renault in 1974 from Citroën) all are now marketed internationally as Renaults, though the individual names remain in their homeland for the time being. Several models use the Club of Four cab, whilst normal-control Saviems are MAN-based, as are several of Renault's diesel engines. Some Alfa-Romeo van models are based on Saviem designs, the Ford Transcontinental uses a Berliet cab shell, and Mack's medium-weight trucks are produced for them by Renault, who acquired a 20% stake in the American firm in 1978. Renault Véhicules Industriels make approximately 50,000 commercial vehicles per year, and double that number if assembly outside France is added, and employ some 35,000 in France.

JN 90 from intermediate range of 6- to 13.5-tonne rigid trucks plus artics has 'Club' cab, 9-tonne GVW, and 133 bhp, six-cylinder diesel.

148

GRH 235 (when sold as a Renault or Berliet, **HF 26V** when Saviem) 6×4 for up to 30 tonnes GVW and 38 tonnes GCW. Turbocharged six-cylinder diesel develops 228 bhp and gearbox has eight forward speeds.

TR 305 available like most other models as a Renault. Saviem or Berliet (whose design it originally was) in France. It has a turbocharged, six-cylinder, 300 bhp diesel with 'torque-rise' to minimize gear changing, and is for 35 to 38 tonnes GCW.

HB 17 Saviem and **GC.GF 231** Berliet for up to 18 tonnes GVW and 32 tonnes GCW. The former has a 185 bhp, six-cylinder diesel whilst the latter has a 215 bhp, turbocharged version. Six- or ten-speed gearboxes are available.

GBH 260 is one of Berliet's traditional normal-control models for GVW of up to 32.5 tonnes and GTW up to 80 tonnes. It has a 217 bhp, six-cylinder, normally aspirated diesel. Other versions are available with 6×6.

REYNOLDS-BOUGHTON

Reynolds-Boughton Chassis Ltd
Winkleigh Airfield
Winkleigh
Devon EX19 8DR
England

The Boughton Group

Boughton has made forestry and agricultural
equipment—notably winches—since the last century,
whilst Reynolds specialized in the supply of off-road
conversions of proprietary chassis, notably for export,
in the fifties and sixties. The two then combined to make
crash tender chassis which are fitted with fire-fighting
equipment and bodywork by such specialists as Carmichael, Gloster Saro, Angloco and Chubb in the UK
and by Rosenbauer in Austria. 4×2, 4×4 and 6×6
models are produced and in 1978 Reynolds-Boughton
added a general-purpose, 5-ton GVW, 4×4 using certain
Ford A components.

RB 510 4×4 is for 5 tons GVW and can have Ford, Perkins or Bedford petrol or diesel engines of 85 to 138 bhp.
The cab is a modified version of the Ford A Series.

Pegasus chassis equipped by Chubb as their Spearhead model has rear-mounted, Rolls-Royce, 235 bhp, petrol engine driving all four wheels via an Allison automatic transmission. Top speed is 100 km/h (62.5 mph) and 400 gallons (1800 litres) of water are carried within a GVW of 7 tons.

Taurus 6×6 chassis for 28 tons GVW undergoing tilt test. It has a rear-mounted, Detroit V-12 diesel developing 525 bhp, Boughton gearbox, Kirkstall bogie and 10,000-litre (2200 gallons) tank capacity. Top speed is 100 km/h (62.5 mph) and a larger Griffin version for 37.5 tons GVW is produced with Detroit V-16, 608 bhp diesel and Scammell bogie.

RFW

The RFW Truck Manufacturing Corp
56 Boundary Road
Chester Hill
NSW 2161
Australia

Although several British and American manufacturers build trucks in Australia specially for local conditions, RFW were unusual when they started in 1969 in that they were a locally owned company. Their first vehicle was a 4-axle tipper using a Scania engine and Bedford cab. More recent productions have used purpose-built cabs and can be built to any specification, including various off-road 6×6 models. Engines by Cummins, Detroit, Caterpillar, Rolls-Royce and UD Nissan are offered from 200 to 550 bhp. The firm was started by Robert F. Whitehead, hence the initials.

RFW **6 x 6** tipper has RFW-built, PermAtrak, 2-spring bogie, axle casings and transfer box. Allison automatic, Fuller manual and other transmissions are available and the example shown is Cummins powered. Two, three or four thickness composite chassis are offered.

RIMPULL

Rimpull Corp
Box 748
US 169 South
Olathe
Kansas 66061
USA

As manufacturers of components for dumptrucks Rimpull decided to enter the complete vehicle industry in 1975. It makes rear dumptrucks to 120 tons capacity and bottom dump articulated coal haulers to 170 tons. All feature mechanical, as opposed to diesel-electric drive and have the unusual feature of a radiator mounted behind the cab, where it provides a positive head of water, is away from dust and does not interfere with driver's visibility. The Rimpull name is derived from a special drive axle developed over 30 years which gives a claimed 40% extra torque at the wheel rim thanks to a double reduction planetary arrangement in the wheels and double reduction in the differential housing.

WT 15 water tanker has 15,000-gallon tank interchangeable with dump body and is for laying dust on haul roads (it can cover a seven-mile road 70 ft wide in 20 minutes and one load) or can be used for firefighting. It can have six-cylinder Cummins or V-16 Detroit diesels of approximately 600 bhp and six-speed Allison automatic transmission. A 20,000-gallon version is also available.

154

ROBUR

VEB Robur-Werke Zittau
Strasse der Einheit
Zittau 860
German Democratic Republic

The East German state-run commercial vehicle factories produce various models from the front-wheel drive, Renault engined, Barkas one-tonner to 18-ton artics based on the IFA rigid five-tonner. The industry is currently being reorganized and modernized with help from Volvo. The Robur name was first used in 1956 on a replacement for the ageing Phänomen air-cooled engined truck models.

Robur models are for up to 3000 kg loads and can have 4×2 or 4×4. The engine is a four-cylinder, 3345 cc, air-cooled, 55 kW (75 bhp), petrol unit with five-speed gearbox (plus two-speed auxiliary in 4×4 version).

SAURER

Adolph Saurer Ltd
9320 Arbon
Switzerland

Having made their first car in 1896, Saurer turned their attention to heavier vehicles and produced a 5-tonner in 1903. This and their following designs proved so successful that several other European manufacturers built them under licence, and a factory was established in America, which finally merged with Mack. Saurer were amongst the earliest firms to produce a diesel-engined commercial vehicle and today are Switzerland's largest heavy-vehicle maker, also producing similar vehicles with a Berna nameplate, Berna having made commercial vehicles since 1904. Saurer-Berna also have technical and commercial ties with Fiat's OM truck subsidiary, whose lighter vehicles they sell in Switzerland with Saurer or Berna badges. On the passenger side they have links with DAB, who assemble buses in Denmark and are associated with British Leyland.

D 330 8×4 for 32 to 36 tonnes GVW has six-cylinder, 330 bhp, turbocharged diesel of 12 litres capacity and nine forward gears.

156

D 290 has 12-litre, turbocharged, 290 bhp, six-cylinder diesel and is for 19 to 21 tonnes GVW or up to 60 tonnes GTW as ballasted tipper or tractor.

D 290 4 × 4 is mechanically similar to 4 × 2 above but has normal-control with fibreglass bonnet. GVW is 19 tonnes.

SCAMMELL

Scammell Motors
British Leyland UK Ltd
Tolpits Lane
Watford WD1 8QB
England

BRITISH LEYLAND SCAMMELL

Scammell made their first vehicle, a petrol-engined, chaindrive, articulated 7.5-tonner shortly after World War I. They then specialized in off-road vehicles, 3-wheel mechanical horses, maximum-capacity articulated vehicles and heavy-haulage tractors, of which they built the first 100-tonner. Today they continue to make vehicles in many of these categories as well as some more conventional haulage models. They are members of Leyland Vehicles having been acquired by Leyland Motors in 1955. Scammell vehicles are now sold under their own or Leyland's name and they also make developments of two former Thornycroft models, the LD55 Bush Tractor and the Nubian crash tender chassis.

Nubian fire crash tender chassis comes in 4×4 and 6×6 rear-engined versions with Motor Panels cabs and central steering position. They have 300, 400 or 500 bhp Cummins diesels, Allison five-speed gearboxes with two-speed Kirkstall auxiliary box and axles. The example shown has Chubb coachwork and fire equipment.

Commander tank transporter was introduced in 1978 as replacement for Thornycroft Mighty Antar and complements Crusader, Contractor and the new 350 bhp S24 6×4 or 6×6 rigid or tractor. Commander 6×4 can carry a 65-tonne load at 61 km/h (38 mph) and has a Rolls-Royce 625 bhp, V-12 diesel and Allison six-speed torque converter transmission.

LD55 is for 27.7 tonnes GVW and 66 tonnes GCW. It has a Leyland 150 kW (202 bhp), six-cylinder diesel and Fuller five- or six-speed transmission. Its no-frills design is intended for durability and servicing simplicity.

159

SCANIA

SAAB·SCANIA

Saab-Scania
Scania Division
S-151 87 Södertälje
Sweden

Scania's origins go back to the Vabis company, who were building railway carriages from 1891 and who made their first truck in 1903. Scania was producing trucks before 1910 and joined forces with Vabis in 1911. Scania-Vabis trucks continued to be made until 1969, when the Vabis name was discontinued and Scania joined with the Saab car firm to create Saab-Scania. Trucks ranging upwards from 8.3 tons capacity are produced. The first figure in two-figure Scania model numbers indicates the engine capacity in litres, as do the first two figures in three-figures model numbers. Scania has factories in Sweden, Holland, Brazil and Argentina and makes around 22,000 heavy vehicles per year.

LBS141 is for 15.6-tonne loads (plus trailer load) and has 14.2-litre, V-8, 275 kW (374 bhp), Scania turbo-charged diesel. It has 6×2 and ten-speed gearbox with synchromesh.

160

LT146 tractor for up to 120 tonnes GTW has same 14.2-litre diesel and transmission as LBS 141 and 6×4. Its GVW is 34 tonnes and it has hub reduction rear axles.

SBA111 4×4 military truck with 11-litre, six-cylinder diesel developing 149 kW (202 bhp) and two-ratio, six-speed gearbox in which half the ratios are hydraulic and half manual with automatic changing. Load is 4.5 tonnes plus 6 tonnes towed.

SCOT

Scot Truck Ltd
PO Box 70
Debert
Nova Scotia BOM 1GO
Canada

Scot built its first truck in 1972 using American proprietary components and, until 1976, Ford cabs. It then
added forward-control models and conventionals with
its own styling. The firm is owned by the Irving Oil Co,
who run a substantial fleet of Scots. Current production
includes rigid and artic trucks, loggers and other off-
highway vehicles and fire-engines, which are usually
equipped by Pierreville Fire Trucks Ltd, Pierreville, Que-
bec. Scot also builds Cummins 450 bhp engined tractors
for the Canadian army.

6×4 highway tractor is available with various transmission options and 180 to 600 bhp diesels by Cummins, Detroit or others. Extensive use of fibreglass is
made in the cab and bonnet construction.

SD

Shelvoke and Drewry Ltd
Icknield Way
Letchworth
Hertfordshire SG6 1EN
England

SD began in 1921 by making unusual low-loading trucks wiith transverse engines and semi-automatic transmission. These were their staple product until the fifties and were particularly popular as municipal vehicles. In 1946 these were joined by a larger and more conventional chassis, from which has developed a wide range of municipal vehicles. In 1975 SD launched their SPV (special-purpose vehicle) range which includes custom-built trucks for all sorts of on- and off-road uses.

PY has wide version of SD steel and grp tilt cab and is shown here with SD-built intermittent refuse compaction body. It is for 16 tons GVW and has Leyland or Perkins diesels of approximately 140 bhp.

163

NYC 16- ton GVW 4 × 4 with Motor Panels tilt cab, Leyland 144 bhp, turbocharged diesel and six-speed plus two-ratio auxiliary gearbox.

Chubb-SPV 4 × 4 crash tender with rear-mounted Detroit, 430 bhp, V-8 and Allison five-speed automatic gearbox for 60 mph and 27 tons GVW. SD make a wide choice of rear and mid-engined 4 × 2, 4 × 4 and 6 × 6 crash tenders.

164

SEDDON ATKINSON

Seddon Atkinson Vehicles Ltd
PO Box 7 Woodstock Factory
Oldham
Lancashire OL2 6HP
England

After acting as hauliers and commercial vehicle repairers
from 1919, Seddon built their first truck, a 6-tonner
using a Perkins diesel, in 1938. Because it weighed
under 2.5 tons unladen it was permitted to travel at
30 mph in Britain, and this advantage, together with a
low price, led to considerable orders. Over the years they
were successful with many models built to a similar
philosophy. In 1970 Seddon acquired Atkinson who had
made steam wagons from 1916 to 1931 and diesel
vehicles from 1931 onwards. In 1974 the combined firm
was acquired by International Harvester. Seddon Atkinson has a workforce of 2000 and a capacity of roughly
6000 vehicles per year.

200 model for 16 tons GVW has International 5.87-litre
(358 cu ins), six-cylinder, 100 kW (134 bhp) diesel and
Eaton five-speed, constant-mesh gearbox. It has a steel
tilt cab produced in conjunction with Motor Panels which
is lower than the similar structure on the 300 and 400.

165

300 6×4 is for 24 tons GVW in Britain and has a six-cylinder, 7.64-litre (466 cu ins), 145 kW (194 bhp), International diesel and ZF six-speed, constant-mesh gearbox.

400 is available as a 2-axle artic unit or rigid for drawbar trailer work for up to 32 tons GVW in Britain, or as a 6×4 or 8×4 rigid. Various Cummins, Gardner and Rolls-Royce diesels of up to 320 bhp are available. From 1981 the lightweight 401 tractor replaced the above with traditional Atkinson badge.

SEMEX

Semex Nutzfahrzeuge GmbH
4270 Dorsten
Borkener Strasse 52
West Germany

Semex is the West German importer of Tatra and Skoda/
Liaz trucks. It also makes a range of special-purpose 6 × 6,
8 × 8 and 8 × 10 vehicles with Tatra or Deutz air-cooled
diesels. All have low-mounted forward-control cabs
except the 6 × 6 tipper, which uses a semi-forward-control structure from the British firm of Motor Panels Ltd,
Coventry.

26 256 tipper is for 26 tonnes GVW and has a Deutz
V-8 diesel developing 188 kW (256 bhp). The two-
range, five-speed gearbox and the axles are by Tatra and
the Motor Panels cab and bonnet tilt in one unit.

SFB

SFB Spezialfahrzeugbau GmbH
Helmholtz Strasse 9
4018 Langenfeld/Rhld
West Germany

SFB was established by the Bodo Toense Crane Company to make special-purpose chassis for mounted cranes and other heavy-duty transport. They offer various models including 8×4, 8×6 and 12×6 types used by several drilling rig, pile-driver and other equipment makers, including the German end of the American Grove Crane Corp.

SFB **HTL2525-20** drives on all but the middle axle and is available with 285 to 400 bhp diesels. This example is shown carrying a concrete pump and hydraulic 45 m placement boom.

168

SISU

Oy Suomen Autoteollisuus AB
PO Box 10307
Helsinki 10
Finland

As Finland's major heavy-vehicle builder since 1931,
Sisu now make several truck and bus models as well
as such special-purpose vehicles as crane-carriers. They
are associated with British Leyland and use many Leyland components, as well as Rolls-Royce Eagle diesels
in some larger models. Both Leyland and Scania have
a 10% stake in the company.

M–162 6×2 for 38 tonnes GTW is the most powerful
in the Sisu range and has a 370 bhp, Cummins, 14-litre
diesel. Sisu also supply this type of cab to Dennison
in Eire.

SOVAM

Sovam
Chatillon sur Thouet
BP 56
79200 Parthenay
France

Since the early sixties Sovam has specialized in special vehicles for airport cargo loading as well as mobile libraries, shops, ambulances, etc. They have front-wheel drive, which allows a low rear floor height, especially on models with twin rear axles and extra-small wheels.

Typical of Sovam's special vehicles is this 6×2 mobile cinema which extends to double the length shown here, thanks to telescopic body construction. The 2-litre diesel engine and transmission are by Renault.

SPARTAN

Spartan Motors Inc
Charlotte
Michigan
USA

Following the end of production by the original Diamond-Reo company various parts of the firm, plus some of its designs and models, were taken up by other manufacturers. Some of its personnel, suppliers and distributors also became involved in spin-off operations. Amongst these was Spartan in 1975, which made custom-built on- and off-road chassis and fire appliance chassis. By the eighties its annual turnover was two million dollars.

Spartan **CFV** chassis equipped as Custom Pumper by FMC Corp, Tipton, Indiana 46072. It can have various engines by Caterpillar, Cummins or Detroit and Allison, Spicer or Fuller transmissions. A tandem axle version is also produced.

STAR

Fabryka Samochodów Ciężarowych
Starachowice
Poland

Made since 1948, Star trucks were Poland's best known
until the arrival of Jelcz. Today the two factories have
close links and Jelcz bodies many Stars as well as
supplying its French-designed steel tilt cab for some
models, notably the Star 200 150 bhp, six-tonner. Star
has made 6×6 military vehicles since the fifties and now
these are available with Jelcz-type enclosed cab or its
own open design. Annual production is reported to be
25,000.

600 M1 is a 6×6 truck for carrying 4 tonnes and towing
an additional 2½ tons. It has a six-cylinder, 4678 cc,
105 bhp, petrol engine and five-speed gearbox with
two-range transfer box. A waterproofed version able to
wade to a depth of 80 cm is available.

STEYR

Steyr-Daimler-Puch AG
Kärntner Ring 7
Vienna A-1010
Austria

Steyr have made trucks since 1922 and now produce
the small 4×4 Pinzgauer cross-country vehicles as well
as a range of 2-, 3- and, recently, 4-axle trucks. In addition to the vehicle illustrated, Steyr make a range of
lighter, semi-forward-control trucks and 7- and 12-ton
payload 4×4 trucks for off-road and Alpine conditions.
Steyr have close links with Mercedes-Benz. Steyr's ad-
vanced tilt-cab shape dates from 1968 and current production totals 6000 per year, accounting for some 35%
of the heavy vehicles on the Austrian roads.

91 Series trucks all have similar styling and are available
with 4×2, 4×4 (shown), 6×2, 6×4, 6×6 and occasional
8×2/4. Engines range from 6595 to 11,970 cc and
power output from 107 to 235 kW (145 to 320 bhp).
Steyr, ZF or Fuller gearboxes are used.

STONEFIELD

Stonefield Vehicles Ltd
Cumnock
Ayrshire KA18 1SH
Scotland

Founded by the late Jim McKelvie, who introduced
Volvo commercial vehicles to Britain, the Stonefield
cross-country vehicle was developed from 1974, with
some of the prototype work undertaken by Jensen
Motors. It is designed round a flexible space frame using
box-section girders and can have 4×4, 6×4 or 6×6
drive. Various engines can be used and automatic transmission is fitted. The vehicle uses simple assemblies and
widely available bought-in parts to assist overseas
manufacture. The British government owns a 76% stake
in the company and quantity production began in
earnest in 1978 with a target of 2500 vehicles per year.

P3000 has 3-litre, Ford, V-6, petrol engine and P5000
has Chrysler, V-8, 5.2-litre, petrol engine. They develop
respectively 138 and 150 bhp. Both have three-speed
automatic transmission and incorporate the Ferguson
system of positive traction which includes torque pro-
portioning and automatic differential locking. The 4×4
has a load capacity of 1500 kg (3307 lbs) and the 6×4
(trailing rear axle) one of 2918 kg (6432 lbs).

SUTPHEN

Sutphen Fire Equipment Co
7000 Columbus-Marysville Rd
PO Amlin
Ohio 43002
USA

Founded in 1890, Sutphen has a long history of producing fire equipment but it was only in the 1960s that complete vehicles were offered. Prior to that, and to a lesser extent today, commercially available chassis have been used. In 1963 an aluminium, lattice section, telescopic aerial tower was perfected of which hundreds have now been produced, many on Sutphen chassis.

Sutphen aerial tower and 1500-gallon pumper has choice of engines of 265 to 525 bhp, the example shown having Detroit diesel and five-speed manual gears. Sutphen are equipped with Cincinnati steel cabs and tower reach is 78 ft.

TATRA

Tatra NP
742 21 Kopřivnice
Czechoslovakia

The forerunner of Tatra, Nesselsdorf made its first vehicle in 1897 in Austria. After World War I the town of Nesselsdorf was in Czechoslovak territory and its name changed to Kopřivnice. From 1923 its vehicles were called Tatra, after the mountain range. A feature of their design by Hans Ledwinka was a central backbone chassis with swing-axle independent suspension on all wheels and air-cooled engines. These features are retained to this day. Tatra makes 7000–15,000 heavy vehicles per year and assembles lighter Saviem vehicles under the name of Avia (not connected with the Spanish firm of the same name).

815 S3 is a 6×6 vehicle for 26,000 kg GVW and 38,000 kg GTW. It has a V-10, air-cooled, 15,825 cc, 196 kW (266 bhp) diesel and two-range, five-speed gearbox. The steel cab tilts. The engine uses many common components with V-8 and V-12 diesels of up to 199 kW output used in forward-control 4×4, 6×6 and 8×8 models and normal-control 6×6 tippers.

TEREX

General Motors Scotland Ltd
PO Box 27, Newhouse Industrial Estate
Motherwell, Lanarkshire ML1 5RY
Scotland

General Motors produce a wide range of earth-moving equipment in USA, Scotland, Canada, Luxembourg, Brazil, Australia, India and South Africa. The British factory was founded in 1953 when its products were known as Euclid. Following Anti-Trust legislation in the United States (similar to the Monopolies Commission rules in Britain) the Euclid division had to be sold. White acquired it and have recently sold it to Mercedes-Benz. Meanwhile General Motors resumed operations in Scotland under the name Terex, and make a wide range of medium to giant dumptrucks powered by Detroit or Cummins engines. In 1980 the German ZBH group acquired Terex.

Terex **33-07** can carry 36,300 kg (80,000 lb) and has a maximum heaped capacity of 29.4 m³ (38.5 cu yds). It has a 392 kW (525 bhp) gross V-12, 13.94-litre (852 cu in), turbocharged Detroit diesel, and six-speed Allison automatic gearbox. It is suspended on nitrogen/oil cylinders.

TITAN

Titan GmbH
Appenweier
West Germany

The Bauknecht Group had made crane transporter chassis at their Rastatt truck factory until production ended in 1970. In the following year the former design team established Titan to produce similar vehicles. These now include special on-/off-road chassis for cranes and special machinery, and very heavy-duty 8 × 8 road tractors of 600 to 800 bhp for towing cranes and trailers of up to 1000 ton GCW. A recent development has been heavy-haulage tractors based on Mercedes-Benz components. These have 21-litre, 400 bhp, V-12 diesels and ZF automatic gearboxes. GTW is 180 tons and the 6 × 6 chassis have Mercedes forward-control cabs.

Titan **KT 25.64/66** is a 6 × 6 chassis for transporting construction machinery to off-road sites. It has a 230 bhp diesel engine.

TOYOTA

Toyota Motor Sales Co Ltd
No 23–22 Izumi 1-chome
Higashi-Ku
Nagoya
Japan

Toyota has made vehicles since 1935. It has expanded rapidly since the 1950s and now assembles vehicles in sixteen countries as well as Japan. Its commercial vehicles are all in the light and middleweight bracket and include off-road utility models as well as buses, trucks and pick-ups. Toyota also controls Daihatsu, who make small car-based commercials and 4×4s, and Hino, who make heavy diesel vehicles.

Toyo-Ace is available in 1.5- and 2-ton capacities with 1994 cc (122 cu ins), 76 bhp petrol, or 2188 cc (134 cu ins), or 2481 cc (151 cu ins) diesels developing respectively 62 and 66 bhp.

Dyna 3-tonner with longest wheelbase can have 2977 or 3576 cc (182 or 218 cu ins) 76 or 89 bhp diesels.

Truck (model name) is largest Toyota for loads of 4 to 5 tons. It has a 4230 cc (258 cu ins), 128 bhp petrol engine or a 6494 cc (396 cu ins), 140 bhp diesel.

UNIC—see Fiat entry

UNIPOWER

Unipower Vehicles Ltd
41 High Street
Thames Ditton
Surrey KT7 0SG
England

Unipower began in 1938 by producing 4×4 road and forestry tractors. Trucks for timber transport remained their speciality until recently when they introduced a range of 4×4 chassis suitable for various specialist off-road duties. Since 1975, they have concentrated largely on fire/crash tender chassis, using Rolls-Royce and Cummins engines. In 1977 the company was acquired by AC Cars Ltd. Unipower is currently completing an order from Japan worth £1 million and exports account for some 90% of its production.

Unipower Model **C44-20** is a 4×4 chassis for 20-ton GVW with Cummins six-cylinder, turbocharged, 365 bhp diesel and five-forward-speed automatic gearbox. This example is equipped by Carmichael of Worcester as their Protector 44U model with 7727-litre (1700 gal) foam-making liquid tanks. Top speed is 96 km/h (60 mph) with a 0–80 km/h (0–50 mph) time of approximately 35 seconds.

VOLKSWAGEN

Volkswagenwerk AG
3180 Wolfsburg
Brunswick
West Germany

Military versions of the 'Peoplescar' were made in World War II and in 1950 a forward-control transporter with air-cooled boxer motor was introduced, of which 5.5 million were made up to 1979, when a new 'Commercial' was introduced. In 1975 VW moved into a heavier weight range with their LT and then collaborated with MAN to introduce a 6–9-tonne GVW range in 1979. In the same year they bought a majority shareholding in Chrysler do Brasil, makers of Dodge trucks in South America.

Commercial can have 1584 or 1970 cc, air-cooled, rear-mounted, four-cylinder, boxer petrol engines developing 37 or 51 kW (50 or 70 bhp). Four-speed synchro or three-speed automatic gearboxes are available, there is independent suspension all round and loads of up to 995 kg can be carried.

LT in unusual guise as a bullion van. LT can have four-cylinder, water-cooled, front-mounted, 1984 cc, 55 kW (75 bhp), petrol engine or six-cylinder, 2383 cc diesel of identical output. Four- or five-speed synchro gearboxes are available and models cater for loads of from 1.25 to 2.5 tonnes.

VW—MAN range covers 6—9 tonnes GVW and this is the largest **9.136** with MAN 100 kW (136 bhp), six-cylinder diesel, VW five-speed synchro gearbox and tilt cab based on LT. Payloads of up to 5650 kg can be carried.

183

VOLVO

Volvo Truck Corporation
Truck Division
S–405 08 Göteborg
Sweden

Volvo has made commercial vehicles since 1928 and now produces light vans (based on the old DAF Vario-matic—Volvo recently bought DAF's car division) up to heavy-haulage models. They are involved with the Club of Four (Magirus Deutz, Saviem and DAF) with a rationalized mid-weight range, and own Bolinder Munktell, who produce Volvo BM dumptrucks. Volvo own their British sales outlet who also assemble special models for UK use.

Volvo is Europe's third largest heavy-vehicle maker and a pioneer since 1954 of small-capacity, high-output, turbocharged diesel engines.

F4 range is for payload/body loads of 4.4 to 5 tonnes and has Club of Four tilt cab, six-cylinder, 3.6-litre, turbocharged, swirl chamber (to give petrol engine characteristics), 93 kW (126 bhp) diesel. It has a five-speed synchro gearbox. Other trucks between the F4 and F12 are the 5.48-litre F6, the 6.7-litre F7 and the 9.6-litre F10 ranges.

F12 is available with 4×2, 6×2 or 6×4 and shares its steel cab structure with the F10. GVW ranges from 19.5 to 32.5 tonnes and GTW up to 100 tonnes. Its 12-litre, six-cylinder, turbocharged diesel develops 258 kW (350 bhp) and it has an eight-speed gearbox with torque converter or a sixteen-speed splitter box, both with full synchromesh.

N range covers 4×2, 6×2 and 6×4 normal-control models with 5.48-, 9.6- or 12-litre diesels. Shown is the **N10** 6×4 for up to 32.5 tonnes GVW. Its six-cylinder turbocharged diesel develops either 185 or 220 kW (250 or 300 bhp) and it has the same transmission options as the F12.

WABCO

Wabco Construction and Mining Equipment Group
2300 NE Adams Street
Peoria
Illinois 61639
USA

Originally RG LeTourneau earth-moving equipment and
then LeTourneau-Westinghouse. Wabco is an abbrevia-
tion of Westinghouse Air Brake Corporation, who are
now part of the American Standard Company. Wabco
make some of the largest trucks in the world, using
engines normally found in railway locomotives and
electric drive on the heavier models. The Haulpak range
first appeared in 1957 and now covers 35–235-ton payload capacities.

Haulpak 170C is largest Wabco 2-axle model and is
for loads of up to 154 tonnes (170 US tons). It has
diesel-electric drive using a V-16 Detroit engine developing 1600 bhp and hydro-pneumatic suspension.

WALTER

Walter Motor Truck Company
School Road
Voorheesville
New York 12186
USA

William Walter built his first car in 1898 and from 1911 specialized in trucks. His son saw the inability of 4×2 trucks to work off the road in France during World War I and returned to develop 4×4 trucks which featured automatic-locking and torque-proportioning differentials to minimize wheel slip. These became popular for off-road transport and snow ploughing and updated versions are still in production. During World War II Walter added airport crash tenders to its range and over 1000 are currently in service in airports around the world with a variety of proprietary engines.

Rapid-1 is designed to reach airport fires rapidly and extinguish or contain the blaze until larger crash tenders can reach the scene. It can reach 50 mph from standstill in 18 seconds and has a top speed of 76 mph. The machine has 4×4, a 321 kW (430 bhp) diesel and a GVW of 10,063 kg (22,185 lbs).

Model C has twin rear-mounted diesels totalling 373 kW (500 bhp) and carries 500 gallons of foam and 3000 of water. Turret nozzle delivers up to 1500 gpm and GVW is 27,669 kg (61,000 lbs).

Walter makes a variety of 4×4 utility trucks suitable for snow ploughing. Several types of engine can be specified and all share with the crash tenders the special feature of three automatic locking differentials for positive traction and dead axles with independent shaft drive to reduction gearing in each wheel.

WARD LAFRANCE

Ward LaFrance International
Elmira Heights
New York 14903
USA

The LaFrance family began to make fire equipment a century ago and now two separate fire-engine specialists, Ward LaFrance and American LaFrance, bear their name. The former has made various types of chassis since World War I and now produces military, airfield and fire-fighting vehicles including 8×8 transporters for the US and Moroccan armies. Ward LaFrance is also the exclusive distributor of Maxim Industries fire apparatus.

Patriot custom pumper has steel tilt cab, pumps from 750 to 1250 gpm, with a tank capacity of 500 to 1000 gallons. Top speed is 60 mph. The standard engine is an International gas (petrol) unit but the example shown is one of a batch of 110 for the USAF with Detroit 6V-53 diesels and Allison automatic transmission.

WERKLUST

Machinefabriek Werklust BV
PO Box 159
Kanaal Zuid 114
7332 BD Apeldoorn
Netherlands

Werklust has produced special vehicles for the construction industry since 1974 as well as wheeled loading shovels since the late forties. Its first trucks were front-wheel drive, 3-axle, skip loader/transporters, which were followed by off-highway dumptrucks, in which Fodens took a marketing interest.

WD 3 is a pivot-steer, 30-tonne capacity dumptruck available with 6×4 or 6×6. It has a six-cylinder, 6.99-litre, Detroit diesel developing 189 kW (257 bhp) and Allison automatic transmission with four speeds forwards and backwards. There is reduction gearing in the hub of each driven wheel and balance-beam rear suspension with Metalstik bearings. Top speed is 45 km/h (28 mph).

WHITE

White Truck Group International
PO Box 91500
Cleveland
Ohio 44101
USA

White's origins were as sewing-machine makers but they built cars and trucks from 1900. All were steam-powered until petrol engines were offered in 1909. White has acquired many famous names in its long history, such as Autocar in 1953. White now makes an extensive range of vehicles in most weight ranges and produces the West Coast Western Star range, first introduced in 1967. White's 1978 production totalled 13,330 and because it lacked lightweight models several European manufacturers including VW and Mercedes-Benz have tried to form links. The most recent was MAN who bought 12.6% of the company but later cancelled plans to increase this to 51%.

Road Boss 2 is available with 4×2 or 6×4 and 210 to 430 bhp diesels, by Caterpillar, Cummins or Detroit. The cab is steel or aluminium with a fibreglass hood (bonnet). Various front axle 'set back' positions are available.

Road Commander 2 has an aluminium tilt cab and various diesel options from 230 to 450 bhp. All fuses and electrical connections are housed in a pull-out drawer in the cab. 4×2 and 6×4 versions are offered.

Western Star Conventional range is produced in Utah and British Columbia for mountainous on- and off-highway West Coast operation, primarily in the logging and construction industries. Numerous engine and transmission options are available and the vehicle construction makes widespread use of aluminium.